Wild Dublin

ÉANNA NÍ LAMHNA is a long-standing member of the panel of experts on RTÉ's wildlife programme 'Mooney goes Wild', and one of the most instantly recognisable voices on Irish radio. Originally from Louth, she now lives in Dublin; she is trained in botany and microbiology and has a H.Dip in education. She has been president of An Taisce since July 2004. Éanna is also the author of several other popular wildlife books.

Dublin Photographer, **ANTHONY WOODS** has worked with Irish and international magazines, advertising agencies and his work illustrates books (*Between the Mountains and the Sea*, 2007; *Eating to Win, Irish Rugby Players' Recipes Revealed*, 2005). Known for his discerning eye and ability to connect with his subjects, he has established himself as a well-respected artist. In *Wild Dublin* he often catches the attention of the animals before taking their picture to engage them, thus revealing their character to the reader.

WILD
DUBLIN

Éanna Ní Lamhna

Photographs by
Anthony Woods

THE O'BRIEN PRESS
DUBLIN

First published 2008 by The O'Brien Press Ltd.
12 Terenure Road East, Rathgar, Dublin 6, Ireland.
Tel: +353 1 4923333; Fax: +353 1 4922777
E-mail: books@obrien.ie
Website: www.obrien.ie

ISBN: 978-1-84717-012-5

British Library Cataloguing in Publication Data
Ni Lamhna, Eanna
  Wild Dublin : exploring nature in the city
  1. Natural history - Ireland - Dublin
  I. Title II. Woods, Anthony
  508.4'1835

1 2 3 4 5 6 7 8 9 10
08 09 10 11 12

Editing, typesetting, layout and design:
The O'Brien Press Ltd

Printing: Europrinting S. p. A., Milan, Italy

ÉANNA'S DEDICATION

I dedicate this book to Richard Collins, my friend and colleague.

ANTHONY'S DEDICATION

To my dearest Amanda – thank you for all your support.

ÉANNA'S ACKNOWLEDGEMENTS

I would like to thank the many people who helped me with this book. Niall Hatch of Birdwatch Ireland was generous with data and anecdotes. Eric Dempsey shared his knowledge of unusual bird sightings. Richard Collins gave swan data and checked the veracity of the information. Tom Hayden provided information on Dublin's mammals, particularly the Phoenix Park deer. John Harding accompanied me enthusiastically on my journeys by foot and bike.

I wish to acknowledge the help given by Dublin City Council. The biodiversity officers, Siobhán Egan and Mairéad Stack, were unfailing in their helpfulness in providing maps, documents and papers. Thanks also to Terry Doherty, the Dublin Conservation Ranger and to Rosaleen Dwyer, Biodiversity Officer, Dún Laoghaire-Rathdown.

Help from the following is also gratefully acknowledged: Tina Aughney, Pat Corrigan, Eamon de Buitléir, Terry Flanagan, Billy Flynn, Maureen and Noreen McGuinness, John McLoughlin, Phil O'Malley, Michael O'Meara, David Wall and Ken Whelan.

Síne Quinn did Trojan work editing it, David Daly did the beautiful drawings and Emma Byrne laid it out splendidly. Thank you to Susan Houlden for her helpful suggestions, Natasha Mac a'Bháird for proofreading, Erika McGann for production, Aoife Webb for indexing and Michael O'Brien, publisher. Thanks also to Keith Barrett of Design Image for designing the maps, Trinity College Dublin for permission to reproduce the image from the Book of Kells and Ordnance Survey Ireland for permission to reproduce their map of Dublin. Thank you all.

ANTHONY'S ACKNOWLEDGEMENTS

Thanks to Derek Collins, for coming out on cold nights and windy days in pursuit of pictures. Thanks to Hillary Knox for the tea, biscuits and badgers. Thanks to Richard Collins for showing me the adventurous way to see bird colonies. Thanks to Paul & Mary Clynch for the Mousecapades. Thanks to Pat Corrigan on Bull Island and all other Park and Wildlife Rangers for their advice and help, and to the UCD Fawning team in the Phoenix Park.

O'BRIEN PRESS ACKNOWLEDGEMENTS

The publisher wishes to thank the great and diverse team who helped create, nurture and bring this book into the world: Gerry Barry and his colleagues in Dublin City Council for helping so much; the former City Manager, John Fitzgerald, for believing in the original concept; RTÉ Education for special support; Anthony Woods, a remarkable photographic talent, who gave more than he was asked; Éanna Ní Lamhna for her humour, professionalism and ability to communicate the complexities of nature in a popular style; the design, editing and production talent at O'Brien, who excelled despite daunting pressures.

Dublin City
Baile Átha Cliath

CONTENTS

PREFACE

Everyone knows if you want directions in Dublin City you ask a culchie. They are far more familiar with places in the city than most of the true Dubs. So it is as a culchie that I undertake this task of writing about Dublin City's wildlife – albeit as one who left her native county of Louth forty years ago and has lived here ever since.

Writing a book entitled Wild Dublin is surely an exercise in optimism. Who can ever know or record the presence of every single species? What this book sets out to do is to demonstrate the enormous variety of plants and animals that share our most densely populated urban environment. It has involved researching the immense body of work already published – 'standing upon the shoulders of giants' as Isaac Newton famously said.

There is evidence that the Liffey banks were inhabited as early as 140AD, when the settlement was called Eblana. However, it was when the Vikings sailed up the Liffey in 841AD, and established their settlement Dyflin, downstream from the Gaelic river crossing Átha Cliath, that it became significant. By 988AD the settlement was important enough to be made to submit its rulership to the High King Malachy II. Academic interest in wildlife, however, was far from the minds of those early inhabitants. It was not until 1650 that any observations on Dublin's wildlife were published, when the flower Spring squill – *Scilla verna* – was recorded by John Ray, 'at Ring's – End near Dublin.' Plants were considered worthy of mention in print from then on and there is a body of work on Irish flora that includes many references to Dublin's plants from the eighteenth and nineteenth centuries. Records of Dublin's animal life begin much later – that is if we disregard what poor gullible Giraldus Cambrensis wrote in his 1187 *Topographia Hibernica* about venomous animals not being able to flourish in Ireland. Animal records for Dublin date from John Rutty's publication in 1772 – *An essay towards a natural history of the county of Dublin*.

Each subsequent work builds on what has gone before. New field work is carried out, changes are noted, additions recorded, absences lamented. Dublin City in the twenty-first century is a thriving capital city – yet it is truly amazing how much wildlife is still here.

The photographic eye of Anthony Woods has enriched the book with striking photographs of everything from pygmy shrews to wild orchids, taken over a period of two years. Total dedication is required in order to get photographs of wary urban wild animals. Anthony's photographic missions included camping out in St Anne's Park, scaling rock faces, wading through freezing-cold water, crouching for hours in back gardens, graveyards, woods, harbours and bridges. Not only did he encounter magnificent wildlife, but also came across some fascinating individuals – a walk on the wild side in every sense of the word.

Badgers won't emerge until they are perfectly sure the coast is clear. Full concentration is required to get a photograph. So there was Anthony waiting patiently downwind of the sett entrance, suddenly realising that he was being watched suspiciously by a gang of teenagers in possession of a trolley load of drink. Sometimes discretion is the better part of valour.

Early in the morning, very early, is the time to photograph foxes. So imagine his surprise on being approached at dawn by a man who tried to persuade him to embrace God and return to the fold. When such admonishments were getting nowhere, the man turned away and tried all the car doors in the nearby car park instead. Anthony didn't dare ask!

There were daytime adventures too – photographing seals at the end of Bull Island was such an absorbing task that he didn't notice the swiftly returning tide. Suddenly the water was lapping round his ankles. He had to beat a hasty retreat with all his precious camera gear held high over his head, as the waters rose swiftly up around his chest. And indeed badgers are not even safe during the day in the parks, where he saw people encouraging their dogs – quite illegally – to go down the badger setts. His advice is not to go watching for wildlife alone at odd hours in remote places, the human wildlife might be more than you bargain for!

David Daly's stunning drawings have ensured that the animals that steered clear of Anthony's lenses appear in glorious colour. The Liffey and Dodder otters successfully avoided all attempts to be photographed – so the otter in the Zoo was kind enough to oblige. Mapmaker Keith Barrett of Design Image created clear yet informative maps.

All in all, this book is the result of much cooperation and dedication. I hope that it will help you, the reader, observe and enjoy the surprisingly rich wildlife to be found in Dublin City.

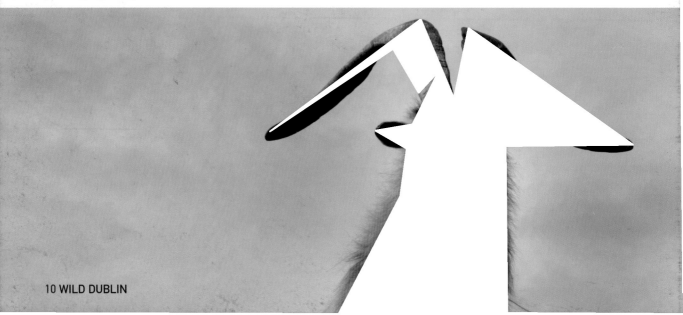

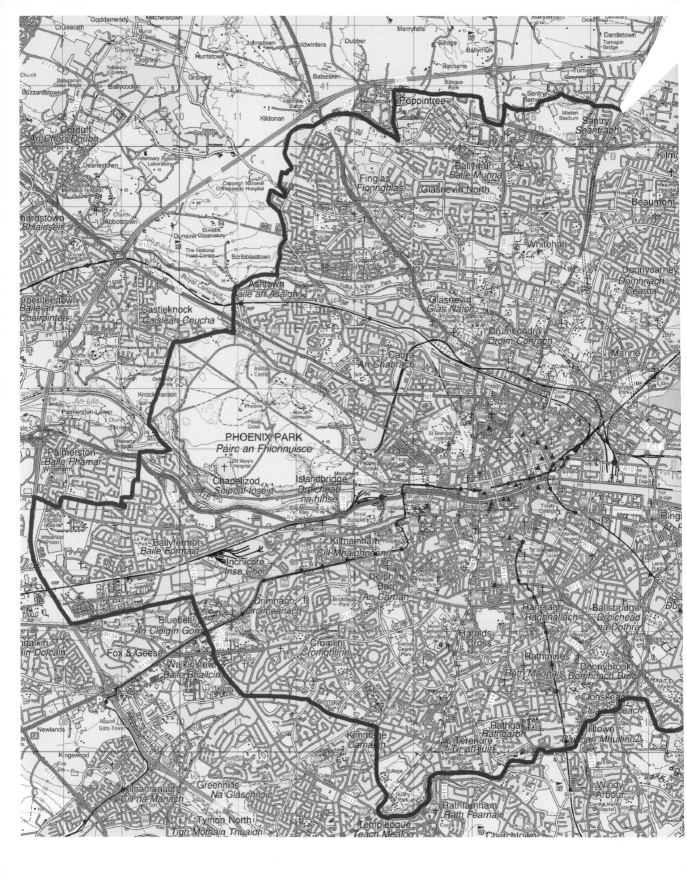

INTRODUCTION

Dublin is a city of over one million inhabitants according to the Central Statistics Office figures for 2006. The urban centre of Dublin City can be defined as the area inside the M50 motorway. This area has the highest density of population in Ireland, with an average of 4,304 persons per square kilometre.

Of these more than half a million live in the Dublin City Council area. The M50 motorway forms a definite boundary to the urban centre of our capital city. The whole of the Dublin City Council area is located here. Small portions of Fingal and South County Dublin districts, as well as Dún Laoghaire-Rathdown, also lie within this apparently arbitrary boundary. However, because this busy motorway forms a definite barrier to the movement of plants and non-flying animals, it is considered to be the boundary of Dublin City, from a point of view of wildlife. On the face of it, it is hardly an area where a huge variety of wildlife might be expected to occur. However, Dublin City contains a remarkable variety of both plant and animal life.

Ireland, because of its geographical location as an island on the north-west of Europe, has quite a small biodiversity of plant and animals relative to larger mainland European countries, and indeed, relative to its larger neighbouring island too. What is amazing is the number and variety of plants and animals that occur within the confines of Dublin City.

Left: Garden snail crossing a quiet road, city centre
Below: South Wall, Poolbeg lighthouse in the distance
Right: Young and mature deer, Phoenix Park

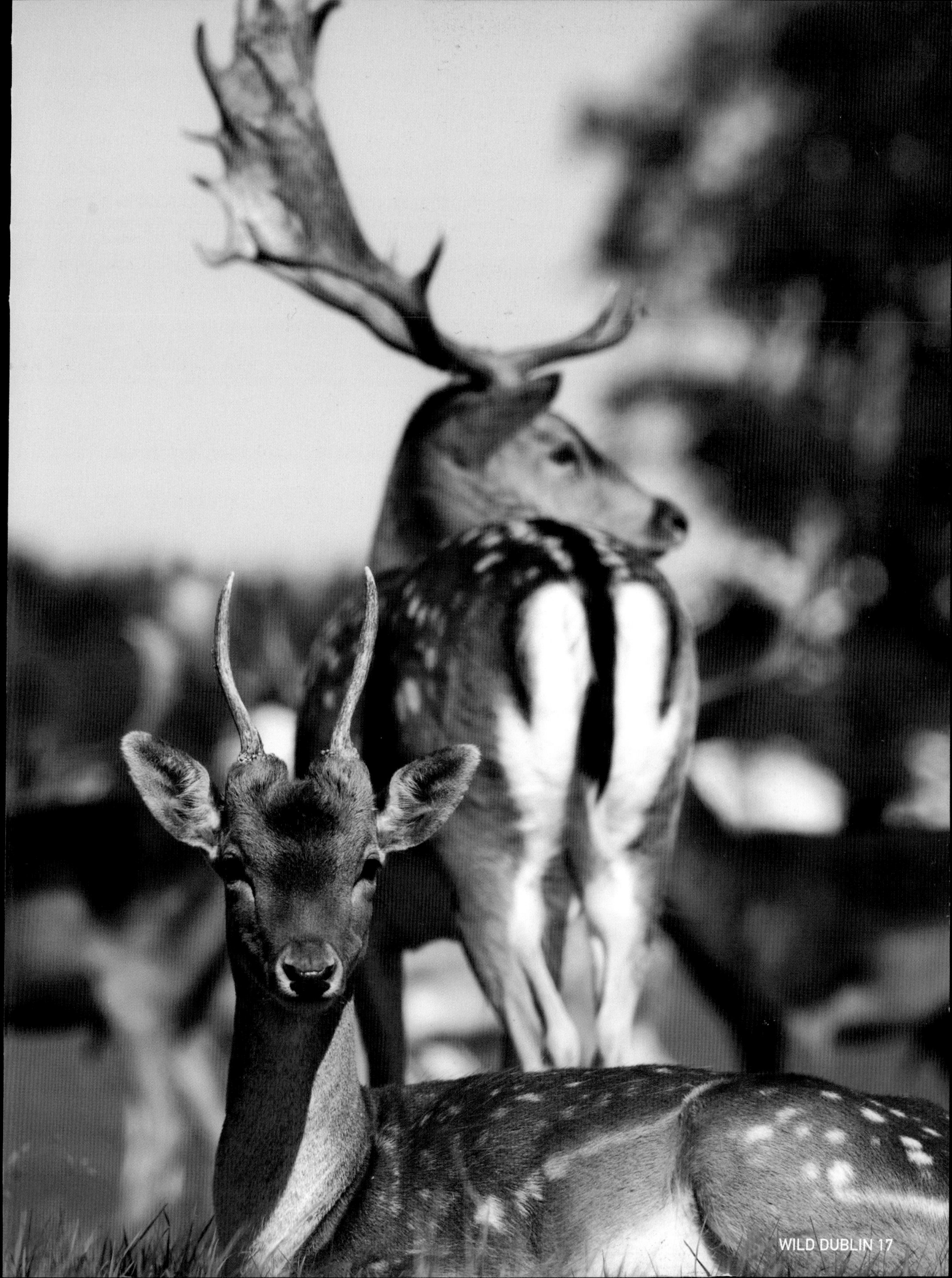

There is an official Irish List of all the wild plant and animal species in Ireland. This list is being continually updated as their distribution changes and the task of doing this lies with the Irish Biological Records Centre in the Institute of Technology in Waterford.

Take our mammals for example, we have a total list of thirty-two land mammals in Ireland. Of these, a remarkable twenty-five species occur in Dublin City (see checklist in Appendix). Another five species of sea mammals can be seen in Dublin Bay.

Birds, of course, are not constrained by vehicles or motorways. There is a total of 450 species of bird on the Irish List. This includes birds that only ever occurred here once or were blown off course during migration and were given the dubious pleasure of visiting our island; of this total 214 bird species have been recorded as occurring in the Dublin City area (see checklist in Appendix).

The other three vertebrate groups of animals are reptiles, amphibians and fish. Ireland boasts only one native species of reptile, the lizard, and it counts Dublin City as a place to live – to the amazement of householders who encounter one in their gardens. We have three amphibian species on the Irish List – of these the frogs and the newts are recorded as part of the Dublin fauna. The Natterjack toad is the only Irish amphibian not recorded in Dublin, as it is a Lusitanian species that occurs only on the Dingle peninsula in Ireland, and then in Spain and Portugal.

Jackdaw perched on sign, city centre
Left: Lizard, Airfield House

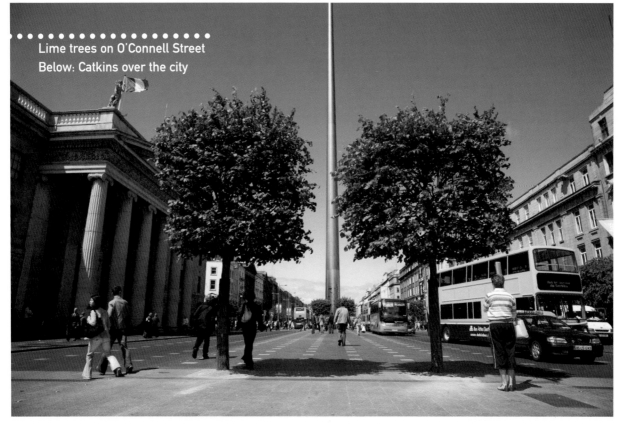

Lime trees on O'Connell Street
Below: Catkins over the city

Two canals (the Royal and the Grand) and three large rivers (the Liffey, the Dodder and the Tolka) as well as a number of smaller rivers flow through Dublin City. The water quality in all these rivers is very good and a wide variety of freshwater fish occur. Native fish such as salmon, trout, eel, stickleback, minnow, stone loach and lampreys all occur (see checklist in Appendix). Rudd, perch, roach, pike, tench, carp and bream have been introduced and are fished for most enthusiastically by city dwellers, who often return them alive.

Dublin lies in the driest part of Ireland and the urban infrastructure, with its concrete brick and stone, raises the temperature to give an urban microclimate, which is somewhat warmer than surrounding non-built up areas.

Chestnut trees along the lakeside, Bushy Park
Below right: Rowan tree

This all has an impact on plant life. Over 1,300 plant species have been recorded for the whole of County Dublin (*Flora of County Dublin*, 1998) and of these 358 species were recorded as occurring between the Royal and Grand Canals during a survey carried out in 1984 (*Flora of Inner Dublin*).

Dublin also has a fine collection of mature trees. Long established buildings have excellent examples of mature trees in their grounds, and indeed some of these remain when the original big house is no longer apparent. The fine stand of yew, arbutus and walnut in the small front gardens of houses on Grosvenor Road is older than the houses in whose gardens they now grow. They are a souvenir of a time when trees were valued, and indeed when developers were careful to leave them intact during building operations.

As might be expected, there are fine specimens of trees in the Botanic Gardens, in the grounds of Trinity College and in the Phoenix Park.

HISTORY OF PLANT RECORDING IN DUBLIN

Irish plants and their distribution have been studied intensively over the last few centuries and several floras have been published. Caleb Threlkeld published a book on the plants in Ireland in 1726, which contains many records for Dublin City. *Synopsis Stirpium Hibernicarum,* (Threlkeld, Dublin MDCCXXVII). Many of the plants he names still occur in Dublin City, growing more or less where they were in his time. He noted wall barley growing around Baggot Street (then called Bagarath). It still grows round there today. Eminent field botanists in the nineteenth century, who also published floras of Irish plant species, such as *Flora Hibernia* (Mackay, 1836) and *Cybele Hibernica* (Moore and More, 1866) included many records of the plants of Dublin City in their work. The Dublin Naturalists' Field Club was founded in 1886 and its members have been active ever since, recording in Dublin City and County.

But it was not until the twentieth century that floras of Dublin itself began to appear. The first of these was written by Nathaniel Colgan, *Flora of the County Dublin* (Hodges, Figgis, & Co, 1904), and it was an exceptionally competent piece of work. Robert Lloyd Praeger, who lived in Fitzwilliam Square, included Dublin records in his published works and worked together with the Dublin Naturalists' Field Club to produce *A Supplement to Colgan's Flora of the County Dublin* (The Stationery Office, 1961). The Dublin Naturalists' Field Club itself got into the publishing business with *The Flora of Inner Dublin* (Wyse Jackson and Sheehy Skeffington, 1984) and *Flora of County Dublin* (The Dublin Naturalists' Field Club, 1998). Both of these books are the results of extensive fieldwork carried out by the Dublin Naturalists' Field Club.

Wild mint

Wild garlic

Green shield bug

There is a wide variety of habitats in the city area where wildlife can thrive quite happily. Private gardens, parks and graveyards all harbour a multitude of species. The coastline has mud flats, saltmarshes, sand dunes and rocky sections. The rivers, canals and various ponds are home to wetland wildlife. There are thousands of different invertebrate species, between marine creepy crawlies and land-living mini-beasts; of our thirty-one butterfly species twenty-five have been recorded in Dublin City (see checklist in Appendix). The fourteen recorded species of dragonfly (out of an Irish total of thirty-three species) are listed; of the twenty-eight woodlouse species occurring naturally in the wild in Ireland, no fewer than nineteen different species have been discovered lurking in various habitats in Dublin City (see checklist in Appendix). There are countless records of bees, wasps, moths, beetles and mayflies, with the evidence, in many cases, on show in the Natural History Museum on Merrion Street. So if it is wildlife you are after, you are in the right place – Dublin City, *Wild Dublin*!

BIOLOGICAL RECORDS

From 1972 until 1988 there was an Irish Biological Records Centre based in An Foras Forbartha, Waterloo Road, Dublin. Here records of mammals, plants and invertebrate groups were collected on a ten kilometre grid system that covered the whole country. Distribution atlases of amphibians, reptiles and mammals, of butterflies and dragonflies and woodlice were published by this centre in the years up to its abolition – along with An Foras Forbartha – in 1988. It was to take more than eighteen years before a Records Centre for Ireland was again set up, this time in the Waterford Institute of Technology in 2007.

The area covered by Dublin City within the M50 falls mainly into four ten-kilometre grid squares – O12, O13, O22 and O23. The species of woodlice, butterflies and dragonflies given in the checklists in the appendix are those recorded in these four ten-kilometre squares.

Checklist – Mammals
Checklist – Birds
Checklist – Freshwater fish
Checklist – Butterflies
Checklist – Dragonflies
Checklist – Woodlice

Orange tip butterfly

Bumble bee

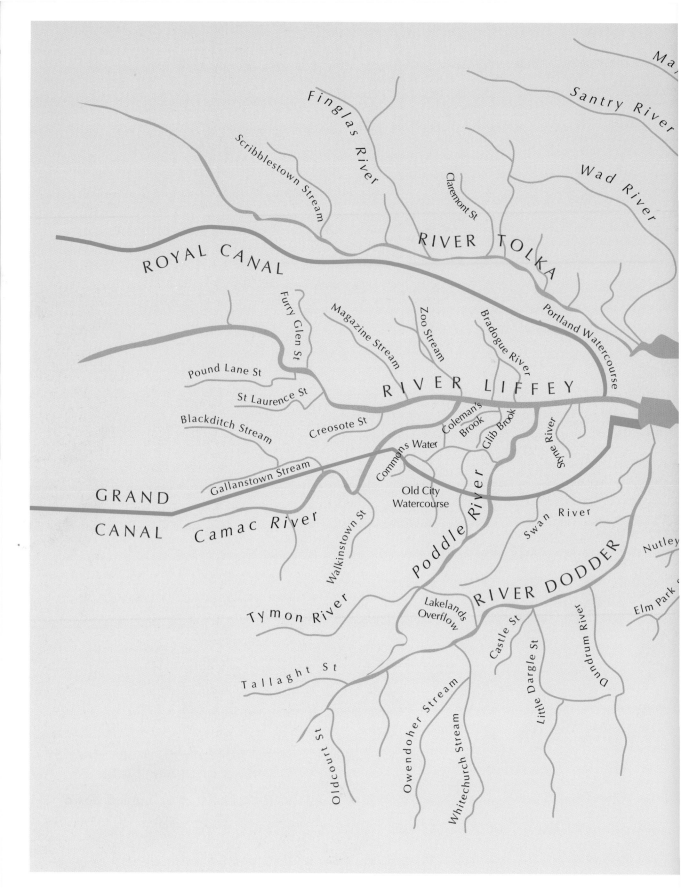

Based on an old map in THE RIVERS OF DUBLIN by Clair Sweeney

Cuckoo Stream

River

Grange Stream

Kilbarrack Stream

Blackbanks St

anniken River

North Bull Island

Dublin Harbour

Dún Laoghaire

eston St

m

Howth Head

Santa Sabina St

Bloody St

Tramway Brook

Gray's Brook

Coolcur Brook

Carrickbrack St

Whitewater Brook

Balsaggart St

CHAPTER ONE

FRESHWATER IN DUBLIN – RIVERS, CANALS AND PONDS

The M50 motorway forms the land boundary of the area covered by this book. It is sometimes so clogged with traffic that it is practically a car park. While travelling slowly on it the opportunity exists to notice how many rivers and canals it crosses.

The first river crossed travelling south is the **Santry River** which flows under the Ballymun Exchange on its way south to the sea slightly north of Bull Island Causeway. It flows through quite a built-up area of Dublin City running through the Stardust Memorial Park and passing through the grounds of St Joseph's Hospital on its way to the north side of the Bull Island Causeway.

The **Nanniken River** is quite a short river and it rises just north of the railway line in Artane. It flows for most of its length through St Anne's Park. In the days when this park was the grounds of a 'Big House' (Thornhill, owned by Arthur Guinness – Lord Ardilaun – from 1834-1925 and accidentally burned down in 1943), the river was widened to form two lakes to add to the amenity value of the grounds.

Liffey Valley Park by Chapelizod

Continuing south, both the **River Tolka** and the **Royal Canal** are crossed at the Blanchardstown Exchange. The Tolka winds its way south from here through Elmgreen Golf Course, Tolka Valley Park, the side of Glasnevin Cemetery and the Botanic Gardens, then down through Griffith Park and past the Archbishop's House, through Fairview Park and into the sea.

The **Royal Canal** is also crossed at the Blanchardstown Exchange – itself no mean feat of engineering – and it keeps company with the railway line right down to Phibsborough. It continues its close liaison with railway lines and sidings, going under the GNR Belfast line and reaching its end in Spencer Dock on the River Liffey.

The **Liffey** itself is crossed by the far too familiar toll bridge whence it flows through Chapelizod, Islandbridge, past Heuston Station and down through the quays and the docks to Dublin Bay.

The M50 crosses the **Grand Canal** just before the Red Cow Roundabout. This canal proceeds eastwards, passing through Bluebell, Drimnagh, Dolphin's Barn, Harolds Cross, Rathmines and Ranelagh to the Liffey at Grand Canal Dock.

The **River Poddle** is crossed as the M50 passes through Tymon Park. It rises naturally and is a natural river that has been culverted artifically, and is fed by some streams from the Greenhills area; it derives most of its waters from the Dodder. Nowadays it does not make it all the way to the sea overground. By Kimmage it is appearing fitfully and by Harolds Cross it has gone beneath the ground. Just before Harolds Cross at Mount Argus, the river was divided in 1491 by a stone divide known colloquially as the 'Tongue', or the, 'Stone Boat'. One third became the old City of Dublin watercourse, while the other two-thirds remained as the River Poddle and continued on to become the

Inset: Tolka River in the Botanic Gardens
Dodder view, Rathgar

original moat around Dublin Castle. However it is now underground all the way from Harolds Cross to the Liffey. It enters the Liffey at Wellington Quay opposite Swift's Row and is intermingled with Dublin's run-off surface water, which is piped into it. It can be glimpsed by the cognoscenti as it flows through a shared culvert in the quay wall.

The **River Dodder** is crossed at the Tallaght Exchange and passes through such leafy suburbs as Templeogue, Bushy Park, Milltown, Donnybrook and Ballsbridge before joining the Liffey at Ringsend. It flows under ten bridges between Ringsend and the Rathfarnham Road, many of which have been rebuilt since their original construction in the 1600s because of floods, which swept them away. Milltown Bridge, however, has been reconstructed because of road widening. The old bridge - Packhorse Bridge - still stands as a pedestrian bridge behind the Dropping Well Pub.

The **Owendoher River** flows under the M50 at Edmondstown and flows down through Ballyboden and Rathfarnham, joining the Dodder at Bushy Park.

The **Whitechurch Stream** flows by St Columba's College and down through the Grange Golf Course and St Enda's Park to join the Owendoher at Willbrook.

The **Little Dargle** is crossed as the M50 skirts Marlay Park. This rivulet traverses Marlay Park and feeds its lakes, but is consigned underground for stretches before it finally flows into the Dodder around Mount Carmel Hospital at Churchtown.

And finally at Carrickmines the **Loughlinstown River** flows into the Dublin area and passes through Loughlinstown and Shanganagh before flowing into the sea, south of Ballybrack.

These rivers are vital wildlife corridors and are responsible for the huge diversity of freshwater wildlife that we have in Dublin City.

Ireland has just two freshwater mammals – the otter and the mink. Both of these species occur in Dublin's rivers.

Huband Bridge (1791) over the Grand Canal at Percy Place

THE OTTER

Otters are at the top of the river food chain and are only present in oxygen-rich waters. If otters are present in a river, it is a sign that the whole food chain is there to support them. This is proof of the good water quality of the river.

Otters are nocturnal creatures; they know only too well the dangers of appearing in broad daylight, so the casual stroller along the riverbank during daylight hours is unlikely to come across one. What is much more likely to be encountered are otter spraints. These black, tarry droppings smell characteristically of fish and cannot be mistaken for dog droppings once smelt. (A small bit of practice will quickly

Otter in Dublin Zoo

make the smeller into an expert!) These spraints are used by the otters to mark their territory and are usually deliberately deposited on grassy mounds, large rocks and on ledges under bridges. This informs other otters that they are passing through claimed territory, and, no doubt, they are probably gender specific as well – interested otters will know if a male or female deposited them. Otter spraints have been recorded under Islandbridge and under Heuston Bridge, at Springfield Bridge on the Dodder and also where the Dodder meets the Liffey at Ringsend.

Otters feed almost entirely on fish – and our Dublin rivers are rich in fish. They have also been known to eat frogs and rats, but they rarely, if ever, dine on waterbirds, such as waterhens and mallard.

Fishermen along the Dodder and the Liffey, above Islandbridge, may sometimes become aware of otters in the water, particularly if they are fishing around dawn or dusk. While out recording for the dawn chorus one very early May morning, I encountered a large otter in the Phoenix Park, running along a park road. It quickly entered the undergrowth and, no doubt, fled back to the pond in the Furry Glen whence it came.

Otters breed in holts – tunnels in river banks. In order to excavate these successfully they use the roots of riverside trees as scaffolding. Large trees with substantial roots are favoured, such as ash, sycamore and horse chestnut. The rivers of Dublin City are part of the linear home range of the otter. The introduction of the coarse fish roach has improved things for the otter, as both adult and young otters feed upon these. There are lots of otters to be seen along War Memorial Gardens on the Liffey. As such, Dublin City is unique among the capitals of Europe for providing habitat for a mammal species listed as endangered on the EU Habitats Directive (Annex 2).

THE MINK

Dublin has the unenviable reputation of being the first place where mink escaped into the wild in Ireland. The mink is a native of North America and was introduced to Ireland in the 1950s for fur farming. It wasn't necessary to have a licence for fur farming in those days and it was not until 1965 that such a licence became necessary. With the advent of such a requirement and a decline in the fur trade ('It takes up to forty dumb animals to make a fur coat and only one dumb animal to wear it', Brigitte Bardot), the number of mink farms declined.

One of the first mink farms in Ireland was set up in 1955 on the Dundrum River behind the then PYE Factory in the village. This did not please the anglers, as the Dundrum River is a tributary of the River Dodder, which is notorious for flooding (it is not called the Dodder – an *Dothra*, meaning turbulent or violent in Old Irish – for nothing!). Of course the very first winter the mink farms were there, there was a great flood down the Dodder and up the Dundrum tributary and all the cages with the mink were swept downstream to They duly escaped into the wild and are inh of the Dodder ever since.

A mink is about half the size of an otter – centimetres from nose to tail; as opposed t centimetres for a male otter. Mink are in the system too and so they can occur along the anywhere they feel secluded enough. They like flowing waters with thick vegetation along banks. It is a solitary animal – males and fem hold their own separate territory while yo mink, which do not yet hold territory, wand through the territory of others. Mink a opportunistic aquatic carnivores, which means th they will kill and gobble anything they can grab. S as well as eating fish such as perch and eel an trout, they will dine happily on rats, mice, frogs waterhens, coot and whatever ducks and ducklings they can surprise.

• • • • • •
Mink

Pussy Willows on the Dodder

Spring is a particularly good time to get out for a walk along Dublin's waterways. It is possible to walk along the Dodder for most of its length from the M50 to the sea and both of the canals are traversable to the public from one side or the other, and indeed on both sides for some of their length in the city. The Grand Canal flows under the motorway, just above the eighth lock, while the Royal Canal flows under the M50, just below the twelfth lock. Both are traversable on foot all the way to the Liffey. The Liffey is bounded by quays up as far as Heuston station, but a lovely walk along its length, further west, is possible on the north side along Liffey Valley Park, and on the south side at Palmerstown through Waterstown Park and further down at War Memorial Gardens in Islandbridge. The River Tolka flows through a golf course, Tolka Valley Park, which has been sensitively developed by Dublin City Council, the side of Glasnevin Cemetery and the Botanic Gardens and so is bordered with a great variety of trees.

Early spring is the time to see the catkins – the flowers that come on the trees before the leaves, as their pollen is wind blown and leaves would only get in the way. Willow, hazel, poplar and alder all have lovely catkins – the downy ones on willow are referred to as 'pussy willows' as they resemble a cat's tail. All of these trees are well adapted to growing along the water's edge and will suffer no harm if they endure the odd

Grand Canal between
Ranelagh and Rathmines Bridge

Anthony Woods
with a Giant hogweed
on the banks of the
River Tolka

flood. As spring advances, these trees will be used by the birds that frequent our waterways.

Later on in the year, the flowering plants appear along the banks. While most of these, such as, reeds and rushes, grow along the edges of ponds and lakes where the non-flowing water allows them settle and become established, there is one plant whose seeds are carried along by the flowing water and which, therefore, can occur on river banks. This is the Giant hogweed. This enormous member of the Umbelliferae family occurs in places along the banks of the Dodder, Tolka and Shanganagh rivers. A huge, white, umbrella-like plant, it was introduced to Ireland as an ornamental plant in the gardens of the landed gentry. The seeds are carried in the flowing waters of streams, and so it spreads in this way. It can grow into quite dense stands following flooding, when the river waters spread over the adjoining land, depositing the seeds on the soil. Giant hogweed loves floods, and as both the Tolka and Dodder are prone to flooding, conditions here suit the spread of this species very well. This plant causes a problem in the wild because it contains sap, which if it gets on the skin, provokes a photosensitive reaction causing blisters and burns to appear on the skin when exposed to sunlight. Therefore great care should be exercised if trying to get rid of this plant, to avoid any sap coming in contact with skin. Use of a strimmer is certainly not advised.

Kingfisher at Dodder Weir

Cormorant on Islandbridge on the River Liffey

Kingfishers are the quality mark of any river. They feed entirely on fish, nest in holes in the bank and need perches over the water to watch for passing fish, because, strange as it may sound for a bird that dines only on fish, kingfishers cannot swim. Our Dublin rivers all boast kingfishers, and a glimpse of one flashing its vibrant colours under a spring sun as it darts up river from bridge to bridge, is a thrilling reward to the city naturalist. Kingfishers are recorded on the Dodder at Bushy Park, on the Tolka at the Botanic Gardens and on the Liffey between Chapelizod Bridge and Islandbridge. Dippers and Grey wagtails are river birds that also can be spotted by the astute. A pair of Grey wagtails nest under the bridge on the White River at St Enda's Park in Rathfarnham. And they are common all along the length of the Dodder downstream from Rathfarnham. They are common too along the

Tolka, particularly along the Botanic Gardens stretch and in Drumcondra. Dippers are small birds the size of blackbirds that feed on the creepy crawlies that live under stones in rivers. To get at them the dipper has to walk along the riverbed against the flowing water, picking with its bill under the stones. Naturally, it can only do this where the water is shallow, otherwise it would drown. Look out for them where the water flows over rocks and weirs, because, while fast moving, it is shallow in these places. Watch out for dippers too in the Dodder at Ballsbridge or at Drumcondra Bridge.

Cormorants, which are familiar as seabirds, have taken to feeding along the Dodder and are quite often seen by observant Luas travellers as they cross the Milltown viaduct. A cormorant is often seen perching on the red-brick chimney on the city side of the bridge.

Walking along quietly, paying attention to small movements, the sharp-eyed observer may well notice – as did the mole in that well-loved classic *The Wind in the Willows* – 'A brown little face with whiskers. Small neat ears and silky hair. It was the Water Rat'. A very affable fellow he was indeed in the story and he took the mole along on a picnic, carrying a basket which famously contained 'coldchickencold tonguecoldhamcoldbeefpickledgerkinssaladfre nchrollscresssandwichespottedmeatgingerbeerl emonadesodawater….' In fact, the picnic basket and its contents, however unlikely, are the only things we can authentically recreate on the banks of Dublin's waterways. We have no moles in this country and there is no such thing as a water rat. What is so lovingly described by Kenneth Grahame in the classic book is in fact a water vole – the European Water Vole *Arvicola amphibius* or *A. terrestris*. This creature occurs in waterways in Britain but not here. No, any rat-like creature that we may happen to spy scurrying along the bank or swimming in the water is the ordinary Brown rat *Rattus norvegicus*. It's not a water rat, just an ordinary rat that went swimming. And they do indeed occur on our waterways. They can carry diseases – fatal to humans – such as Weil's disease so give them a wide berth – you don't want to share any picnic they've been nibbling at.

However, if the intrepid naturalist is rummaging in buildings down on the Liffey Docks where the ships come in and berth. For here – apart from Lambay Island – is the only known Irish haunt of a different smaller species of rat – the Black rat – *Rattus rattus*.

Freshwater habitats are very important to the eight species of bat found in the capital. The Blessington Basin, the River Dodder and the Furry Glen in the Phoenix Park, are some of the best water locations to spot bats. (More information on bats in chapter three.)

Brown rat in Bushy Park

THE BLACK RAT

This rat, also known as the ship rat, is probably the rarest mammal in Ireland now, although at one time it occurred in abundance. It was brought to Ireland by foreigners in boats, hence its Irish name – *Francach* – the French one. Interestingly, the first record of it can be seen in Trinity College, because there is a drawing of it in the Book of Kells, which was written in the eighth century.

Climate deterioration after that made it scarce in Northern Europe – so it didn't accompany the Vikings in their longboats. It was Medieval times before it came to Ireland again and it came in abundance then. It is associated with the Black Death, commonly believed to be the Bubonic plague, which is carried by a bacterium in a flea carried by the Black rat. The rats lived in such close proximity to people in the cities that the fleas jumped from them on to humans, bit them and transmitted this deadly disease. By Christmas 1348 it had killed 14,000 people – a goodly proportion of the population of Dublin city. It took until 1550 for the population of the city to get back to its pre-plague level.

Nowadays it is thought that the Black Death wasn't Bubonic plague at all but a disease spread by a very contagious virus, as Black Death was rampant in Iceland but they never had Black rats. They are digging up old plague graveyards in other countries to see if they can establish what the people died of. Dublin victims of the Black Death were buried in the Black Pits (hence the name), but there are no plans to exhume them.

The Black rat is not called a ship rat for nothing

Black rat, Book of Kells

and supplies of it can come into Dublin port on a ship at any time. During the 1930s 14,000 Black rats were killed in Dublin port. However, with the improvement in ship design and more vigilant pest control, it is very rarely seen in Dublin port – only one record in 2006.

The Black rat is smaller than the common Brown rat. It leaves greasy fur marks on ropes and walls along its runs, which the Brown rat doesn't do, and so a positive identification can be made of its presence if these are seen. Nobody is really keen on going out to look for them or indeed wants to find their presence.

This rat was eventually ousted by a bigger and stronger rat – the Brown rat – *Rattus norvegicus* – its official title. This rat was introduced here in the 1720s, by accident of course, and it quickly out-competed the Black rat. Lambay Island is the only place the Black rat remained as a breeding population. It was last recorded there in 1988, when its bones were found in the pellet of a Short-eared owl. People anxious to make these rats' acquaintance should visit the Natural History Museum on Merrion Street, where stuffed and mounted ones are on display.

Dublin's rivers and canals are surprisingly full of fish – surprising, that is, to those who think that surface litter is the same as water pollution. Fish need oxygen-rich water and no sewage is pumped into any of Dublin's waterways so they have a low Biological Oxygen Demand (BOD). BOD is high when a large amount of organic matter must be broken down by bacteria, leaving no oxygen for other water-dwellers. Dublin's waterbodies are free of organic pollution and are great habitats for fish – both salmonid, other native and introduced coarse species.

Salmonid fish – the trout and salmon – need particularly clean water. The River Liffey has always been famous as a place where the first salmon of the year is caught. It is an exceptionally early river in that some of the first salmon of the year, returning from the ocean to breed, arrive in Dublin Bay in November. These adult salmon begin their return journey up the Liffey to their spawning beds in December. The river has over 1,000 wild salmon a year. It also holds stocks of wild Brown trout and Sea trout.

Salmon

SALMON FISHING ON THE LIFFEY FROM ISLANDBRIDGE TO LUCAN

Islandbridge is a favourite spot for salmon fishing and this area usually produces the first salmon annually. Best times are in the early spring, when the sea adults, known as grilse, are swimming up river and also from June to August. Most Liffey salmon are taken on spinners or worms, while the Sea trout can be caught on flies.

Fishing on the Liffey is controlled by angling associations or private owners. There is free fishing at War Memorial Gardens above Islandbridge. The Dublin and District Salmon and Trout Anglers Association has extensive fishing water on the river at Islandbridge, at the Strawberry Beds along the lower Lucan Road, the Wren's Nest and at CPI Limited.

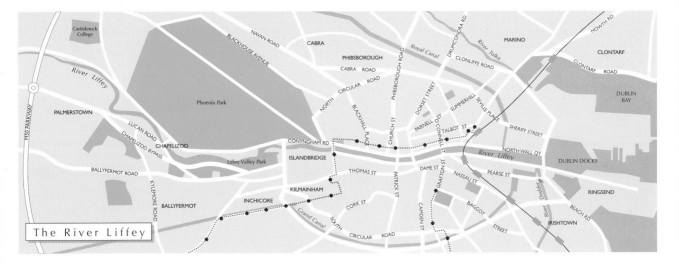

The River Liffey

Liffey from Chapelizod to Islandbridge

WILD DUBLIN 39

RIVER DODDER

The Dodder has only the odd stray salmon, but there is a good run of Sea trout in the lower reaches. The stock of wild Brown trout is exceptional and is complemented by stocking. The best of the Brown trout fishing is between Old Bawn in Tallaght and Ballsbridge. The best of the Sea trout fishing is to be found downstream of Ballsbridge. The local club stocks the river annually with Brown trout from 113g to over 450g. There is a high juvenile membership in the club and young anglers are encouraged to join. Recommended stretches are Herbert Park in Ballsbridge to Beaver Row in Donnybrook, and from Milltown to Rathfarnham. The Milltown to Rathfarnham section is very accessible, with a linear park all the way along this stretch with footbridges across the river at various points. The lower reaches can be good for Sea trout in the late summer. In the tidal area near Ringsend some fine specimen mullet were recorded in recent years. Fishing on this river is controlled by the Dodder Anglers and by riparian owners.

Dodder Weir by Rathfarnham Bridge

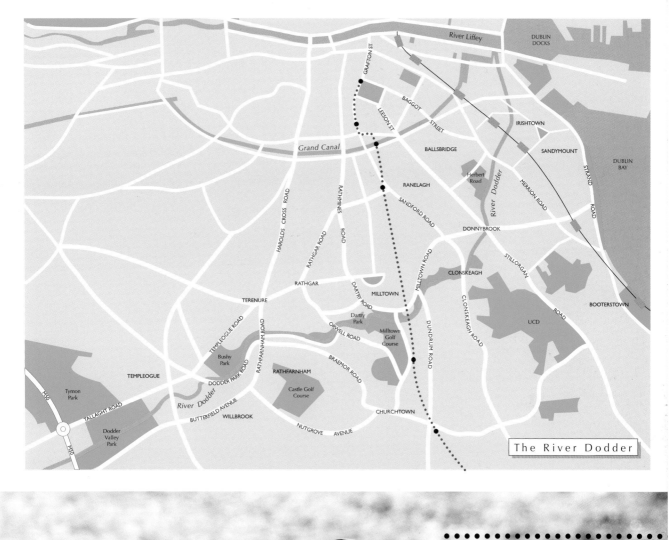

The River Dodder

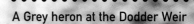

A Grey heron at the Dodder Weir

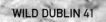

Tolka Valley Park

RIVER TOLKA

The River Tolka in north Dublin is an extremely rich river, which holds some wild Brown trout and some Sea trout. It is mostly a 'put and take' fishery and is stocked by the local angling club, who have permits available. The best fishing is from Finglas Bridge to Abbotstown Bridge. Access is mostly on the northern bank with the exception of a pedestrian footbridge from Ballyboggan Road on the southern bank of Tolka Valley Park. The river supports hatches of olives (young mayflies), midges, gnats and a small hatch of sedge. Some Sea trout fishing is available on the lower reaches of the river. Fishing on this river is controlled by the Tolka Trout Anglers Club and by riparian owners.

All information on fishing Dublin's waterways is available on the Eastern Regional Fisheries website www.fishingireland.net

Other native species of fish in Dublin's waterways include the eel, which is not content just to reside in the rivers but traverses the canals as well and has even been found in the pond in Herbert Park.

The River Tolka

● ● ● ● ● ● ● ● ● ● ● ● ● ● ● ● ● ●
Alder tree by the River Tolka

EELS

Eel are catadramous fish, which means that the eels feed and grow fat here in our freshwater systems, but breed and are born in faraway seas. Eels first become apparent as elvers, tiny worm-like creatures two or three inches long, that appear in the rivers and canals in spring. They arrive in from the sea and, in the main, swim upstream. But if the going gets tough they are not averse to stopping swimming, and getting out and walking, or at least slithering across the wet grass to an adjoining pond. They can climb up the canal locks as there is always a trickle of water coming down these and some plants growing there, which supports them on the climb.

They come out at night from under their stones in the water to feed on whatever insect larvae they can find, and spend the summer days lying motionless, apparently sunbathing, no less. They spend long summers in our rivers and ponds, feeding and growing. They soon change from the tiny glass elvers to yellow eels, which are not so good to eat. They take years and years to grow up. Given that they are three years old when they arrive, they will spend at least another nine years, if they are male, or twelve, if they are female, before they reach puberty. They hibernate each winter, in the mud in the bed of the rivers, and emerge again each April to continue the growing process. As they approach maturity a great change comes over them. They become fatter, their eyes grow bigger and their skin changes colour from yellow to a purplish black. They are now known as silver eels and they are remarkably good to eat at this stage. Dubliners are not too fond of them, but in London jellied eels are now prized as a delicacy, although they were once known as 'poor man's food'.

Having fed and grown fat in our fresh waters for years and years, the adult eels are now overcome

Grand Canal by Clanwilliam Place

with an urge to swim down river towards the sea. They enter the salt water and they never feed again. The fat they have put on is their fuel for their journey all the way across the Atlantic to the Sargasso Sea in the Gulf of Mexico. And it is there among the seaweeds that they mate and die. It must be, because that is where the baby elvers come from, although the adult eels have never been actually recorded breeding there.

There are eels in the Dodder. They travel upstream as far as Firhouse Weir and they climb up the damp mosses by the edge of waterfalls to get to the Rathfarnham stretches.

They occur in the Liffey too where a sexual separation seems to occur, like in the ballrooms of yore. Males stay downstream and only females go far upstream. In December of the year the first baby eels arrive in Dublin Bay from the Sargasso Sea. Some stay around the estuary where there is a record of one 76 centimetre-long eel being caught under Butt Bridge in 1985. Most of the females settle down upstream of Islandbridge Weir. They also occur in the Tolka, in the Royal Canal and the Grand Canal.

Eel

STICKLEBACK

Salmon, Sea trout and eels journey between freshwater and sea each year. But Dublin's waterways have their own resident native fish that stay at home all their lives and are true Dubs. The three-spined stickleback breeds in freshwater and there are resident populations in the canals as well as in the Liffey, Tolka and Dodder above the saltwater level. The adults can feed in the salty stretches too so the grown-ups can be found anywhere along the whole length. They are quite aggressive and hold territory, so they only occur in small groups in the breeding season – the brightly red-coloured male and his small harem of carefully selected females.

Stickleback

Minnow

STONE LOACH

The Stone loach is another very small introduced fish species, which feeds at night in the dark bottoms of our waterways. They have three whisker-like barbels or feelers around the mouth to help them grope for food in the dark. They like fast flowing water.

MINNOW

The minnow has been resident in Irish waters since the 1600s when they were introduced here from Britain. They were known as penks in Elizabethan English and as they are very small fish, they became known here as little penks – pinkeens. They swim in large shoals in summer, when they breed. They swim up near the surface and are the main food of the sharp-eyed kingfishers.

Stone loach

LAMPREY

There are also lampreys in Dublin's rivers. Lampreys are parasitic fish – as adults they clamp onto living fish and suck their sustenance out of them through enormous jaws (although they don't actually kill them). There are three species of lamprey in Ireland: the Brook lamprey, the River lamprey and the Sea lamprey. The Sea lamprey feeds at sea and only returns to our rivers to breed. We don't eat them in this country, as they do in Portugal and France, so there is really no interest in them among our city fishermen. The Brook and River lamprey hold on to stones in the riverbed to prevent themselves being washed away downstream. The Brook lamprey only feed as juveniles on dead plant and animal material. As adults they do not feed at all, but move stones around with their strong jaws to make hollows to lay eggs in. The River lamprey holds on to stones too in the rivers, but they can let go and clamp on to a passing trout, as they do feed as adults in our freshwater rivers. Searches under suitable stones in deep stony parts of our city rivers would produce records of the latter two species. The Brook lamprey is definitely in the Dodder and both Brook and River lampreys are in the Liffey.

All our Dublin waterways are great habitat for coarse fish: rudd, perch, roach, pike, tench, carp and bream have all been introduced and fishing for them is extremely popular along the canals and the three main rivers. While some of these species are edible and make fine eating, if cooked carefully, it is more usual for most coarse fish to be returned to the water and left for the otters, mink, cormorants, herons and kingfishers to feast on.

DUBLIN'S FRESHWATER PONDS

Dublin has freshwater ponds too, and while most of them are small, they provide a different habitat to flowing water. From the air, the biggest area of freshwater is Stillorgan Reservoir, where wildlife is actively discouraged, as this is a holding area for fresh water for the citizens of Dublin City.

Our larger parks all have ponds – some were established as garden features when they were part of the environs of the associated big house – fine examples can be seen in Airfield, Marlay Park, St Enda's Park, Bushy Park, Terenure College Grounds and the pond at Farmleigh in the Phoenix Park. The Phoenix Park also has the Zoo pond and the lake that until recently was part of the grounds of Áras an Uachtaráin, as well as the ponds in the People's Park, the Citadel Pond, the Glen Pond, Quarry Lake and the Machinery Pond. Blessington Basin, in the centre of the city, attracts its own wildlife, as does the pond in St Stephen's Green. There are small ponds in St Anne's Park and several water holding areas in the two golf courses on Bull Island. There are ornamental ponds in Ranelagh Gardens, Herbert Park, Carysfort College and Gort Mhuire, while the Belfield pond, established in 1970 as a water

Reedmace (also called bulrush), Airfield House grounds

supply in case of fire, is now frequented by avian wildlife.

While some of these ponds are supplied with water from a flowing stream, the main characteristic of a pond is that the water is still and there is less naturally-occurring dissolved oxygen in it than in a flowing river. As a consequence it is easier for water plants to become established. The water along some stretches of both canals flows slowly too and there is much wetland vegetation along the canal banks as a consequence. This is where reed beds and stands of rushes and sedges can grow. There are fine stands of Reed Canary grass *Phalaris arundinacea*, Reed Sweet grass *Glyceria maxima*, and Yellow Iris *Iris pseudacorus* in many places along the banks of both canals. Irises and Common reed *Phragmites australis* grow around the ponds in the Phoenix Park. Ponds that are not too intensively managed can have submerged plants too, such as Canadian waterweed *Elodea canadensis* and the pondweeds *Potamogeton natans* and *P. berchtoldii*. If duckweed, *Lemma minor*, is seen floating on the water surface, it shows that the water is really very slow flowing.

Inset: Sedge in Bushy Park around
the woodland
Main image: Yellow Iris in
Tolka Valley Park

Ducklings in the Tolka River in the Botanic Gardens

Pond bird life includes duck such as mallard, which are beloved of the bread-feeding public and are very tame indeed. Males have vivid green heads in the breeding season, while the female is a utilitarian brown with only a flash of colour on the wing bar – indicating that she had to do all the nesting and incubating. While ducks live on the waterbodies, they nest nearby on islands in the lakes or in dense vegetation close at hand. Some Dublin ducks, however, build nests away from water, such as the one that nested one year in the windowbox on the first floor windowsill of a house on the Merrion Road in Ballsbridge, or the one that nests by the lawn in Leinster House and holds up Dublin's traffic as she walks her ducklings from there across to the pond in St Stephen's Green. The other breeding duck in Dublin's ponds is the Tufted duck, which breeds in Blessington Basin. It can also be seen quite readily in the pond in St Stephen's Green, in Ranelagh Gardens' Lake and on the Grand Canal.

Some waterbirds are common to both the ponds and the waterways and also breed in both. Swans can have nests on rivers and on ponds.

Mallard in St Stephen's Green

DUBLIN'S SWANS

Much work has been done by Richard Collins on the distribution in Dublin City of the Mute swan – so called because it makes no sound, unlike its wild relative, the migratory Whooper swan. Mute swans only began to breed in the city around 1922, when nesting was first recorded. Popular tradition has it that Mute swans were not found on the Liffey prior to 1924, when two swans were released by Oliver St John Gogarty at Islandbridge – an event known as his 'offering of swans'. Gogarty supported the 1921 Anglo-Irish Treaty and became a Senator of the Free State in 1922. During the Civil War he was arrested by the IRA, but he escaped his captors by diving into the River Liffey under a hail of bullets. Gogarty promised to release a pair of

swans on the Liffey in thanksgiving, and commemorated the event in a volume of poetry *An Offering of Swans* (1924). All the swans in Dublin – it is said – are the descendants of Gogarty's pair.

Numbers increased from then until the 1970s when all the viable habitat had been colonised. Breeding numbers have changed little in the city since. All the nest sites have been located and mapped and the owners of the nests ringed with easily read white rings. In the area covered by this book there are at least twelve nest sites for the Mute swan. These are on the Liffey, Royal and Grand Canals and in parks such as Bushy Park, Tymon Park and Blessington Basin.

Inset: Cygnet and cob in Bushy Park
Main image: A mature cygnet in Bushy Park

OTHER WATERBIRDS

Other waterbirds include the shy moorhen and the raucous coot. This latter bird is heard before it is seen, and is distinguished from the moorhen by its white head. Coot breed on the ponds in St Enda's and in Bushy Park, while the moorhen is much more widespread along all the waterways. Little grebe also breed in Bushy Park pond. Grey herons stalk the shallows of both ponds and waterways, waiting patiently for a meal of fish or frogs, or indeed they are not above grabbing unfortunate ducklings or even goldfish. They breed in heronries at the tops of tall trees. Ten pairs breed annually in the woodlands at Bushy Park. The herons in the Phoenix Park are apparently able to read, as they turn up every day at the Zoo just when it's feeding time for the sea lions and penguins. Crowds of people assemble to watch the antics of the sea lions and crowds of herons arrive in the nearby trees. At the appointed hour the keeper comes out with a bucket of fish and kind-heartedly flings the odd one to the ever-vigilant herons. They are very commonly seen on all the city's waterways and indeed flying along using the rivers and canals as flypaths – unmistakeable with their broad slow wing flaps and their long legs trailing out behind them.

Coot in Tymon Park

Main image: Moorhen in St Stephen's Green
Inset: Moorhen eggs on the Grand Canal

Inset: Pond skaters in the pond at Airfield House

Frog in the pond at Airfield House

AMPHIBIANS – FROGS AND NEWTS

Two of our three Irish resident amphibian species, frogs and newts, occur in Dublin City. Frogs seem to have been introduced to Ireland in the 1600s. No bones older than a few hundred years have ever been found in this country. The story goes, and is given credence by luminary Robert Lloyd Praeger in his book *The Way That I Went*, that frogs were introduced to Trinity College by Dr Gwithers – a fellow of Trinity – who was doing a study of the quadrupeds of Ireland in the latter part of the seventeenth century. Having failed to find any frogs while doing his baseline study, he introduced frogspawn to the ditch in College Park and from these college-educated frogs all the frogs of Ireland are descended. It should be relatively easy to ascertain by DNA studies if all our frogs are closely related – but do we really want to question a good story by looking for facts? Certainly there is no lack of frogs in the city. They only need ponds to mate and lay eggs in. Once they have done this in February, and the frog spawn is fertilised, their duties as parents are over, and they quickly disperse from the ponds to live in long grass, feeding rapturously on flies and slugs and endearing themselves to gardeners. Frogs can live for up to twelve years, and each spring they emerge from hibernation and make for the pond where they were born, to mate and lay eggs. Tadpoles are food for fish, and indeed herons, so ponds and rivers well inhabited with fish will inevitably end up with very few frogs. Small

Above right: Frogspawn in the pond at Airfield House
Below right: Tadpoles in the pond at Airfield House

fish-free ponds are the place to look for frogspawn and there are plenty of these in city gardens.

There are frogs in the grounds of Airfield House as well as newts in one of their ponds. This latter amphibian arrived in the water when the pond was being established as a teaching resource in recent times. It is the only species of newt native to Ireland – the Smooth newt *Triturus vulgaris*. This creature hibernates nearby during the winter and returns to its pond in spring to mate. This usually takes place in April and newt eggs are different to frogspawn – they are laid singly and are wrapped up in the leaves of plants. They hatch out into tadpoles in the water, but adult newts never lose their tails and resemble lizards in shape, although they are much smaller. After mating, adults leave the pond and hide under stones and pieces of timber by day. At night they emerge to feed on worms, slugs and insects. They themselves, however, are on the menu for lots of creatures higher up on the food chain. Adult newts are preyed on by hedgehogs, stoats and rats, and the tadpoles are food for fish, water beetles and dragonflies.

The third Irish amphibian is the toad. The Common toad does not occur in Ireland at all although when people find a particularly large or warty specimen of frog they sometimes think they have found a toad. However, a simple check will quickly establish that it is a frog. Make it move and it will quickly hop away. It must be a frog because toads can't hop – only walk. Our native toad is the Natterjack toad and it only occurs on the Dingle and Iveragh peninsulas in Kerry. And of course being a Kerry species it doesn't content itself with walking – it runs!

Newt on a leaf in the gardens of Airfield House

INSECTS AND OTHER CREEPY CRAWLIES

Dublin's waterways and waterbodies support a good collection of insects and other invertebrates. The most glamorous water insects are the dragonflies and their smaller relatives the damselflies. These strong flying colourful insects are carnivores and catch smaller insects on the wing. They fly up and down the canals in particular as they can rest on the tall reed vegetation along the banks. Dragonflies and damselflies spend much of their lives as larvae in the water and they can only live in oxygen rich water. So their presence as adults is a good water quality indicator.

Anyone who has ever dipped a net into a pond to catch creepy crawlies will be aware that quite a variety of insect life can occur there. What a few dips with a net produces by way of species can tell you very quickly what state the water is

Four-spotted chaser

in. Top of the list are the pollution-sensitive species. If the oxygen content of the water is reduced because of decomposing organic matter, these species cannot occur. As well as the aforementioned dragonflies, mayflies and stoneflies are in this category and these are to be found in our canals, in the river in St Enda's Park and in the pond at Airfield, among others. Next down on the list are those not so picky species, who can tolerate some diminution in water quality. Among those are water shrimps, which swim around sideways, and the waterlice, which are close relations of the terrestrial species that inhabits our gardens, the woodlice. Things are getting bad if you can find nothing better than leeches − several species of which lurk in Dublin's waterbodies − although none remotely large enough to affix themselves on to us. The last stage before complete destruction of water quality is indicated by bloodworms, which have haemoglobin in their blood to help them to hold on to oxygen, and rat-tailed maggots − the young of hoverflies − which have a long siphon − like a snorkel so that they get oxygen directly from the air. No creepy crawlies at all is a bad sign, but there are very few stretches of waterway in Dublin City that have no wildlife at all.

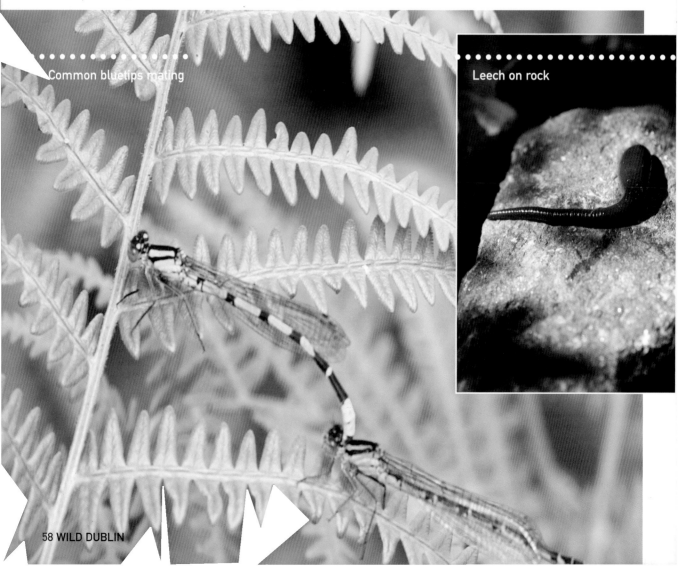

Common bluetips mating

Leech on rock

DUBLIN'S DRAGONFLIES

Dragonflies have been studied and recorded in Ireland since 1846 when the first publication appeared. In 1978 the first Irish distribution atlas was published and in this were records of twelve dragonfly species for Dublin City. Since then a comprehensive survey of Irish Dragonflies – *DragonflyIreland* – has been carried out and the results published in the book *The Natural History of Ireland's Dragonflies* by Brian Nelson and Robert Thompson (2004). This states that there are thirty-two species of dragonfly and damselfly on the Irish list. It confirms that the following fourteen species have been recorded for Dublin City:

Damselflies

Banded jewelwing – *Calopteryx splendens* (pre-1980 record)

Common spreadwing – *Lestes sponsa* (pre-1980 record)

Azure bluet – *Coenagrion puella* (1980-1999 record)

Variable bluet – *Coenagrion pulchellum* (1980-1999 record)

Common bluet – *Enallagma cyathigerum* (1980-1999 record)

Common bluetip – *Ischnura elegans* (1980-1999 record)

Small bluetip – *Ischnura pumilio* (1980-1999 record)

Spring redtail – *Pyrrhosoma nymphula* (1980-1999 record)

Dragonflies

Amber-winged hawker – *Aeshna grandis* (2000-2003 record)

Moorland hawker – *Aeshna juncea* (2000-2003 record)

Spring hawker – *Brachytron pratense* (pre-1980 record)

Four-spotted chaser – *Libellula quadrimaculata* (pre-1980 record)

Common darter – *Sympetrum striolatum* (2000-2003 record)

Vagrant emperor – *Hemianax ephippiger* (Recorded October 1913).

Common darter

The Vagrant emperor dragonfly was apparently spotted resting on the grass in Herbert Park, Ballsbridge by A. Douglas on 12 October 1913. Having never seen such a thing before, he immediately caught it, killed it and sent it off to experts for determination. It turned out to be only the second record in either Britain or Ireland for this species – a sub-Saharan, middle-eastern and Indian species. It has never ever been recorded in Ireland since. But the record is a true one because the specimen was presented to the Natural History Museum where it remains to this day – proof positive of the record.

Above: Common darter
Left: Common bluetip, male

CHAPTER TWO

ACRES OF TAR AND CEMENT – HARD DUBLIN

More than fifty per cent of Dublin City is covered with a hard surface. One might think that the capital's streets, pavements, walls, buildings and bridges, endlessly patrolled by crowds of people and never-ending traffic, must surely be an inhospitable place for wildlife to live. There appears to be little by way of plant life except for street trees and weeds bursting from cracks in old walls or neglected chimney pots. Yet there are many wildlife species which have adapted themselves extremely well to life in such an artificial habitat.

St Stephen's Green

CITY BIRDS

PIGEONS

The most obvious wildlife in the city centre is the pigeon. Anyone with the slightest interest in moving things can't fail to notice their courtship display. The male – all puffed up and important looking – bows repeatedly to an apparently disinterested female who walks away from him, too fast for him to catch up, but she doesn't fly away either. And come evening time they are a familiar sight roosting together on ledges, huddled up against the cold.

Dublin's feral pigeons are descended from the wild rock dove of sea cliffs. They see our city as a collection of tall cliffs and convenient ledges and they breed here in their thousands. Herbivorous birds by nature, they have no trouble finding food in our city and you'll often see them being fed in parks at lunch time. They nest in hollows and sheltered places in buildings, raise two young in each brood and can have up to four broods in a year. Like their wild ancestors they prefer to perch on hard surfaces – statues' heads being a favourite spot.

Pigeon, grounds of Trinity College

See no evil ... pigeons in Irishtown

Peregrine falcon in the Dublin City
Below: Liberty Hall

PEREGRINE FALCON

In turn, pigeons on sea cliffs are food for Peregrine falcons and Dublin City has its very own Peregrine falcons, which prey on the city's pigeons. One was recorded hunting off the Central Bank for unsuspecting pigeons in Dame Street during the summer of 2007. Headless pigeons seen on the ground around St Patrick's Cathedral are the remains of meals eaten by another Peregrine falcon, who perches there.

A few years earlier, the cameras which monitor the city's traffic picked up sightings of a Peregrine falcon hunting around the Liffey area, using Liberty Hall as its base. Members of Birdwatch Ireland got permission to go on to the roof of Liberty Hall to examine the pellets of undigested bits, which would be disgorged by the falcon. These would provide proof of what it had been feeding on. Imagine their surprise when, as well as bits of very dead pigeons, they found clearly identifiable remains of ... woodcock!

WOODCOCK

The woodcock is a wading bird that lives in woodlands and probes in the ground with its long bill for earthworms and insects. We have a native population and indeed the woodcock was one of the birds used on our original Irish coinage. It featured initially on the farthing and then more recently on the fifty pence coin. Our native population is augmented in winter by woodcocks which leave the frozen ground of European forests and fly west to enjoy our warmer winters. Those that featured on the Peregrine's menu were crossing Dublin at altitude, coming from Russia, and were intercepted by the sharp-eyed predator who flew *upwards* to seize them.

Aerial shot of
Dublin City

PIED WAGTAILS

Pied wagtail

The Pied wagtail has traditionally exploited the extra warmth that the city exudes on winter evenings. Flocks of these birds roosted during the winter nights in the plane trees in O'Connell Street, north of the GPO. Christopher Moriarty recounts the story in his book *Exploring Dublin, Wildlife, Parks, Waterways* (Wolfhound, 1997). The use of the trees as a roost in winter began in 1929 when a party of about a hundred wagtails was noticed. This continued every winter – the wagtails arriving in October when the clocks turned back and departing from their roost in mid April. Numbers increased every year until 1950 when a maximum of 3,600 wagtails were recorded. The winter temperature in O'Connell Street can be as much as two degrees warmer than in the surrounding countryside, where these birds feed on insects and spiders by day.

Numbers declined gradually after that and by the late 1990s the flock was down to between 300 and 500. O'Connell Street was completely transformed for the millennium with the erection of the Spire and the replacement of the old plane trees with small-shaped lime trees. So you won't spot any more wagtails roosting on our main street, but small parties of them have been seen roosting in trees in the streets surrounding O'Connell Street. One hundred and fifty were recorded on 11 January 2007 on the trees at the O'Connell Street/Bachelors Walk junction just north of O'Connell Bridge.

SWIFT

A bird that is truly at home in central built-up Dublin is the swift. This migratory bird is the very last one to arrive in Ireland – usually reaching Dublin City by the middle of May. Suddenly one fine summer evening there it is screaming across the sky, heralding its safe arrival from the southern side of Africa. It is also the first to leave as well – it is usually gone by 15 August. This amazing bird is so well adapted to an aerial life that its legs have become weakened from lack of use. If a swift were to land on the ground it could never take off again, so it takes great care not to do so. It can eat, sleep and even mate while in flight but it must make some other arrangement for laying an egg and rearing young. It lays one or two eggs per pair on the bare soffit boards of tall Georgian buildings. There is no nest, as it cannot gather nesting materials on the wing in the hard urban environment. It feeds the young on the aerial insects it snatches from the city skies.

Swallows and house martins make nests from mud – the house martins build them on the outside of houses, up under the eaves, and the swallows build them inside in farm buildings, so neither of these are birds of hard city surfaces.

STARLINGS AND SPARROWS

City buildings are also nest sites for two other city birds – the house sparrow and the starling. Neither of these are really welcome visitors in occupied buildings – particularly the noisy starling with its messy nest of sticks. In fact, one enterprising city starling managed to gain entrance beside a badly-sealed waste pipe and built a huge nest in the casing surrounding the bath in the bathroom inside. The loud objections when the owner drew a rare bath led to their detection, but the kind-hearted house-owner permitted a stay of execution and waited till the young had fledged before calling in a proper plasterer.

House sparrows have become quite scarce in Dublin in recent years. They have gone from the city centre but they are still found in residential areas such as Phibsborough and the Liberties. The male is easily recognised with its black bib and white cheek patches, while the female is brown with white underneath and, unlike any similar sized female finch, has no wing bars or patches. They build untidy nests of dried grass in holes in buildings and can have up to three broods of up to five young in each between April and August. They were formerly extremely common in the city, when they earned a living from the nosebags and droppings of the many city horses.

● ●

Right: A sparrow in St Stephen's Green
Inset: A starling, Merrion Square

HERRING GULL

Other, even noisier, birds have taken to our city roof tops. Due to a population explosion among Herring gulls, there is a lack of nest sites on their traditional breeding grounds on Lambay Island. So it is not really surprising that they have taken to frequenting nearby Howth village, building their nests on the chimney pots. What is surprising is that they have also staked out areas of central Dublin and have begun nesting, in recent summers, on the roofs of the tall buildings in Nassau Street, opposite Trinity College. They scavenge on city scraps and are well able to adapt to the city life and hold their own in food fights for sliced pan on the pond in St Stephen's Green.

BARN OWL

According to Dublin birdwatchers, the city has been the scene for many tales of the unexpected. One incredible story is the well-attested sighting reported by a passenger waiting for the DART in Pearse Street station in the middle of the day. There was a tremendous shower of rain and as he gazed at the roof of the station he beheld a sopping wet barn owl fly in and perch high up under the roof. It crossly re-arranged its bedraggled feathers and resumed the sleep that had been interrupted by the sudden downpour. Who would ever have thought that a barn owl – a rodent hunting bird of farmland – would seek shelter from a storm in a railway station in Dublin City?

A Herring gull, on roof top off Pearse St

MAMMALS

THE URBAN FOX

The city centre is home to birds that feed on aerial creatures or that scavenge food left by careless humans. But there are mammals who live by scavenging too and one such is the urban fox. There is a fox in the city centre, which rejoices in the prestigious address of 1 Grafton Street. It lives in the garden of the Provost of Trinity College and patrols Grafton Street at night, making its way as far as St Stephen's Green, if necessary, in search of food. Foxes are more abundant now in urban areas than they are in the countryside. The average urban fox territory can be as low as 20 hectares, whereas it can be up to a 100 hectares in rural areas.

Urban foxes aren't in the least bit picky about what they consume – they scavenge in dustbins, feed on abandoned hamburgers and chips, grab any unfortunate pigeon that has nodded off on a low window ledge and gobble any mice or even rats that they come across. The Dublin populace generally regards urban foxes with tolerance – which is more than can be said for Dublin's other two commensal species – the House mouse and the Brown rat.

Fox, Raheny

MICE

House mice are in Ireland since the Iron Age and probably have been in Dublin City since its foundation. Mice try and gain entrance to houses in winter and feed on anything they can find about the place. They can quickly become a problem when one considers that females begin to breed as early as six weeks of age. They have up to ten litters a year, with between five and eight young in each litter, and they can easily live for two years indoors. That's 160 offspring over the lifetime of one mouse – YIKES! When you consider that each mouse may produce as many as fifty faecal pellets a day perhaps it is best to stop the mathematical calculations. It is only lack of available food as we become more hygienic in our food habits that keeps them from overwhelming the city.

BROWN RAT

This urban dweller came to Ireland from Eastern Europe in 1722 and by 1730 had become a serious pest in Dublin City. They quickly ousted the Black rat and took over the city, occupying sewers, refuse tips, grain stores, yards and stables – anywhere they could find food. They eat a wide range of food and scavenge meat, fish, bread, bones, grain and vegetable remains. They are very wary of food they haven't had before and only take it in very small quantities, thus it is very hard to kill them with rat poison. Brown rats harbour a number of organisms, which can cause disease to humans. Among these is the bacterium *Leptospira*, which causes Weil's disease. When one considers that up to fifty per cent of Brown rat excrete this in their urine, it is no wonder we welcome creatures like foxes and barn owls, which number them in their diet.

A feral cat in the city

There are no wildcats in Dublin City or indeed in Ireland – you'd need to be in the Scottish highlands for that. However, there are lots of cats that live an entirely independent existence on our city streets – feral cats. Like foxes, these scavenge where they can, kill mice and rats, raid dustbins and, sadly, hunt by day on any young unwary songbird they can find. Foxes are probably their only enemy – the liver of a young cat is said to be a delicacy on the fox menu!

INDOOR INSECT PESTS

COCKROACHES

Rats and mice aren't the only creatures that disturb householders when they encounter them. Some residents of the insect world also come between householders and their sleep. People who have been abroad come back full of wariness about a most unwelcome insect – the cockroach. Do we have cockroaches in Dublin City? Well, we do and we don't. Cockroaches are a tropical group of insects and cannot live in the wild in Dublin. Big black ground beetles however can (and do), and when these are encountered indoors they are often described as cockroaches. A huge infestation of these black ground beetles caused a problem in the Navan Road area during the 1960s when hundreds of them crawled into houses, but generally only one or two are encountered scuttling off at night when the light is switched on. They are carnivores that feed on slugs, worms and earwigs – so encourage them outdoors where they belong.

Real cockroaches, on the other hand, do occasionally occur in heated buildings under artificial conditions. A thriving colony of them lived for years in the lion house in Dublin Zoo, having become established there by an accidental introduction from abroad. They are easily recognised by their extremely long antennae, which curve down over their backs. They do not fly, but emerge at night from crevices in the walls of warm buildings in search of food. If they get introduced to Ireland by accident they can survive indoors in heated buildings, but not outdoors. They cause consternation if detected in restaurants – as they can contaminate food.

MOSQUITOES

The other annoying insect that comes between householders and their sleep is the mosquito. This one is indeed native to Ireland and always has been. At the moment it doesn't carry malaria, as the winters are too cold for the malaria plasmodium to survive. We did have malaria however – known then as ague – up to the middle of the 1600s. Oliver Cromwell was the last person of note to die of this disease in these islands. He died in September 1658 in Whitehall, of malarial fever – apparently contracted initially during his Irish campaign. A little Ice Age then followed and malaria – but not mosquitoes – became extinct in Ireland. Mosquitoes can breed in any stagnant water, ponds, puddles, even the waterdish surrounding a flowerpot. So the unwelcome whine of a mosquito on a still August night in Dublin City is not a figment of the imagination; the tell-tale bites the next day will confirm its attack.

FLYING ANTS

In summer on a still and humid day, without warning, hundreds of winged ants suddenly pour forth from cracks and holes in the pavement and take to the skies. This generally causes consternation, not only among the humans who spot them, but among the swifts and gulls, that wheel around the sky in flocks feeding on this aerial feast.

This social insect is abundant in the gardens and parks of our city, where they have nests with up to ten thousand insects living and working together in perfect harmony. The eggs, laid by the queen, are all reared as worker ants until July. Then, presumably because of the warmer summer weather, the babies that emerge from eggs laid at this time become fully grown fertile queens and drones.

In summer, all on the one day – usually a warm windless day – the hundred of new queens and drones (all with wings) will erupt out of all the nests in an area to mate in the skies over the city. The air is black with flying ants that attract hordes of gulls and swifts that circle the sky in a feeding frenzy dining on the hapless lovers. The queens that are mated successfully fall back to earth, break off their wings, which are now surplus to requirements, and go back underground to start a new colony. They are now really abundant in all our city gardens that have created suitable living conditions for them.

Garden ants about to take flight

PLANTS AND BUTTERFLIES

Dublin used to have many derelict sites around the city centre. When the *Flora of Inner Dublin* (Wyse Jackson and Sheehy Skeffington, 1984) was written, waste ground and derelict sites were some of the main habitats for interesting wild plants. Not so now after the intensive ten years of building in the years prior to 2007. However, one of the most typical plants of waste ground – *Buddleia davidii*, the Butterfly bush – is still to be seen all over the built-up areas of Dublin, bursting from cracks in the walls and adorning unused chimney pots. It lives up to its name and supports collections of butterflies such as Small tortoiseshell and Red admiral. These butterflies treat it like a singles bar and gather there in groups to sip the nectar and meet others of their species with a view to forming a relationship. The eggs of both these species are laid on nettles, which are widespread in the city, so it is no wonder that these are our commonest butterflies in the city centre.

Another butterfly species that has become common in Dublin City in recent times, is the Holly blue. This butterfly appears in spring and lays its eggs on the buds of holly trees, a common enough tree in gardens and parks. These hatch out and become adults in the summer time. This second brood lays its eggs on the flower buds of the ivy. These get as far as the cocoon stage before overwintering and emerging as adults in spring. Both these adults look the same, despite their different food plants as caterpillars, and cannot be mistaken when on the wing for any other butterfly species.

Another butterfly attractant that grows happily on the mortar of old walls is Red valerian, *Centranthus ruber*. This occurs in several varieties of red, and in white also, and is well able to put up with the dryness of old stone walls where there is very little soil and moisture – as indeed can the common dandelion *Taraxacum officinale*. This is often seen bursting through cracks in the pavement and sprouting up from corners where small amounts of soil have gathered. Its unappreciated sunny yellow flowers tell us that summer is on the way.

● ●

Dandelion bursting through city pavement

TREES AND LICHENS

Looking down on Dublin City from an aeroplane it seems to be covered in trees. This is thanks to the street planting schemes of our urban councils. However, not all of our trees were planted recently – some are up to two hundred years old and are evidence of the foresight of past generations. Dubliners have always been proud of their trees and many of the finest are mentioned in *Champion Trees – A selection of Ireland's Great Trees* (Tree Council of Ireland, 2005). Did you know that the Silver maple with the greatest girth in Ireland can be found in the People's Gardens in the Phoenix Park while the Botanic Gardens is home to Irish height and girth champion Pitch pine? In fact the Botanic Gardens has a wonderful collection of record-breaking trees, such as its

Tree of Heaven, Black poplar, Swamp cypress, Red pine, Italian alder and the Tibetan hazel – to mention just a few. But why is there an Irish girth-champion Strawberry tree in the grounds of the Berkeley Court Hotel apartments in Ballsbridge – a tree there much longer than any hotel? The reason is that this was the site of the original Botanic Gardens of Trinity College and the tree bears testimony to this. In the grounds of Trinity College itself are two more specimen trees – an Oriental plane and an Oregon maple.

Dublin's trees also bear testimony to the changing quality of Dublin's air. In 1988 a survey of Dublin's air quality (Ní Lamhna et al, 1988) showed that large sections of the centre of Dublin had very poor air quality indeed.

Oriental plane, Trinity College Dublin
Opposite: Strawberry tree, Berkeley Court car park
(former grounds of Trinity Botanic Gardens)

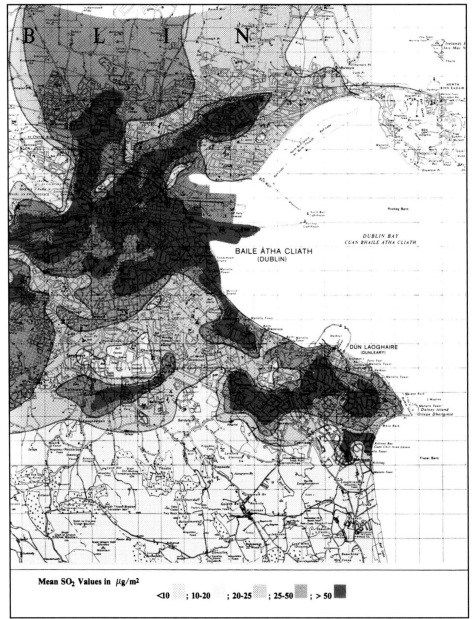

Mean SO$_2$ Values in μg/m^2

◁10 ; 10-20 ; 20-25 ; 25-50 ; > 50

The survey was done by mapping the lichens that grew on the trees in Dublin City. Much of the city centre had trees with no lichens on them at all due to the poor quality of the air. In 1990 the Dublin Clean Air Act forbade the sale of smoky coal in Dublin, and with the subsequent conversion of much of the heating systems to natural gas, Dublin's air became much cleaner. Lichens reappeared on the trees – evidence of the effectiveness of these measures. While there are still areas in the city where, because of traffic emissions, there are still no lichens on the trees, the situation is infinitely better than when all those chimneys – so characteristic of Georgian Dublin – were belching forth smoke from coal fires.

Herring gull, roof top, Ballsbridge

LICHENS

Lichens are organisms which are composed of an algal part and a fungal part. The algal part contains chlorophyll so lichens are able to make their own food by photosynthesis. The fungal part acts as the transport system so that nutrients can move throughout the organism. Lichens have no roots so they are dependent on rainwater for moisture. They are particularly sensitive to pollutants in the air, such as sulphur dioxide and smoke – therefore they are biological indicators of air quality.

They can grow on surfaces such as walls, roofs, gravestones and on the trunks of trees. A good way to obtain an air quality reading is by mapping lichens on the trunks of deciduous trees. Large shrubby lichens grow on trees where the air quality is excellent. Leafy lichens can tolerate some air pollution, while crusty lichens can grow in relatively high levels of air pollution. If there are no lichens on the trees at all this means that the air quality is very bad indeed.

Leafy lichens

Crusty lichens

Leafy lichens on a tree

Crusty lichens on gravestone

Shrubby lichens

In 1988 when the lichen survey of Dublin City was carried out, air quality was so bad that large areas of the city had no lichens at all on the trees. While lichens are now making a welcome re-appearance since the Clean Air Act of 1990, there has been no official survey of them carried out since.

Dublin City Council monitors Dublin's air with the ongoing use of strategically placed monitors and chemical analysis of the results. Dublin's air has improved from a high of 280 parts per million of black smoke in the air during the winter of 1989/90 to less than 20 parts per million in 2004/2005.

So, Dublin's hard surfaces – the acres of tar and cement – have indeed their own very characteristic fauna and flora. If these apparently inhospitable hard surfaces of the built-up city can support such a variety of wildlife then the spaces in between, the parks, gardens and river banks, must be teeming with a wide range of interesting creatures.

Mountjoy Square

CHAPTER THREE

PUBLIC PARKS, PRIVATE GARDENS AND GRAVEYARDS FULL OF LIFE

Dublin was founded by the Vikings, who sailed up the Liffey in 841, and has been expanding ever since. The appearance of the city today and the habitats that exist here for wildlife are the result of the different periods in the growth of the city.

The oldest part of the city is Viking Dublin. The Vikings built their houses out of willow and alder that grew in the flood plain of the Liffey. The inhabitants at that time were not too bothered about encouraging wildlife – they were more concerned with keeping it out. Hedgehogs are the exception as they were introduced to the country by Vikings – as a source of food! The original settlement on the bank of the Liffey had dwellings huddled close together surrounded by city walls.

Medieval Dublin huddled together too – evidence of narrow medieval streets is still discernible today. The wildlife in those times probably lived upon the human person, to the chagrin of the owner. Graveyards were outside the city boundaries, to keep away whatever diseases the occupants died of, as wooden coffins were not too common in those days.

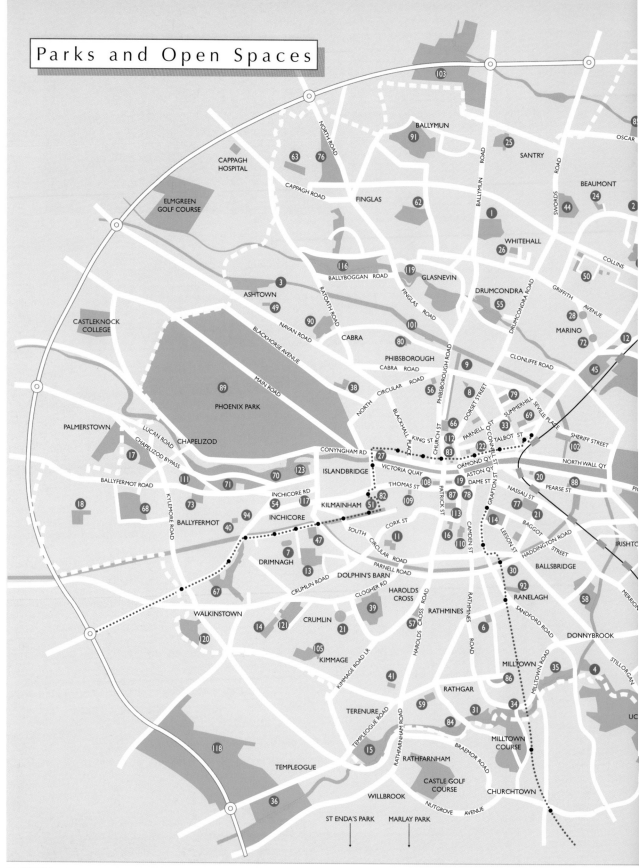

Parks and Open Spaces

BALLYMUN
SANTRY
BEAUMONT
OSCAR
CAPPAGH HOSPITAL
FINGLAS
WHITEHALL
COLLINS
ELMGREEN GOLF COURSE
BALLYBOGGAN ROAD
GLASNEVIN
DRUMCONDRA
ASHTOWN
GRIFFITH AVENUE
CASTLEKNOCK COLLEGE
NAVAN ROAD
CABRA
MARINO
BLACKHORSE AVENUE
PHIBSBOROUGH
CLONLIFFE ROAD
MAIN ROAD
PHOENIX PARK
CABRA ROAD
PALMERSTOWN
NORTH CIRCULAR ROAD
DORSET STREET
SUMMERHILL
SEVILLE PLACE
LUCAN ROAD
CHAPELIZOD
PARNELL ST
TALBOT ST
SHERIFF STREET
CHAPELIZOD BYPASS
KING ST
CHURCH ST
CONYNGHAM RD
NORTH WALL QY
BALLYFERMOT ROAD
ISLANDBRIDGE
VICTORIA QUAY
ORMOND QY
ASTON QY
INCHICORE RD
THOMAS ST
DAME ST
NASSAU ST
KILMAINHAM
PATRICK ST
PEARSE ST
BALLYFERMOT
INCHICORE
BAGGOT
CORK ST
IRISHTO
SOUTH CIRCULAR ROAD
CAMDEN ST
HADDINGTON STREET
DRIMNAGH
PARNELL ROAD
LEESON ST
BALLSBRIDGE
DOLPHIN'S BARN
CLOGHER RD
HAROLDS CROSS
RANELAGH
DONNYBROOK
WALKINSTOWN
CRUMLIN ROAD
SANDFORD ROAD
CRUMLIN
RATHMINES
HAROLDS CROSS ROAD
RATHMINES ROAD
MILLTOWN ROAD
MILLTOWN
STILLORGAN
KIMMAGE
KIMMAGE ROAD LR
RATHGAR
RATHGAR
UC
TERENURE
MILLTOWN COURSE
RATHFARNHAM ROAD
RATHFARNHAM
BRAEMOR ROAD
CHURCHTOWN
TEMPLEOGUE
CASTLE GOLF COURSE
TEMPLEOGUE ROAD
WILLBROOK
NUTGROVE AVENUE
ST ENDA'S PARK
MARLAY PARK

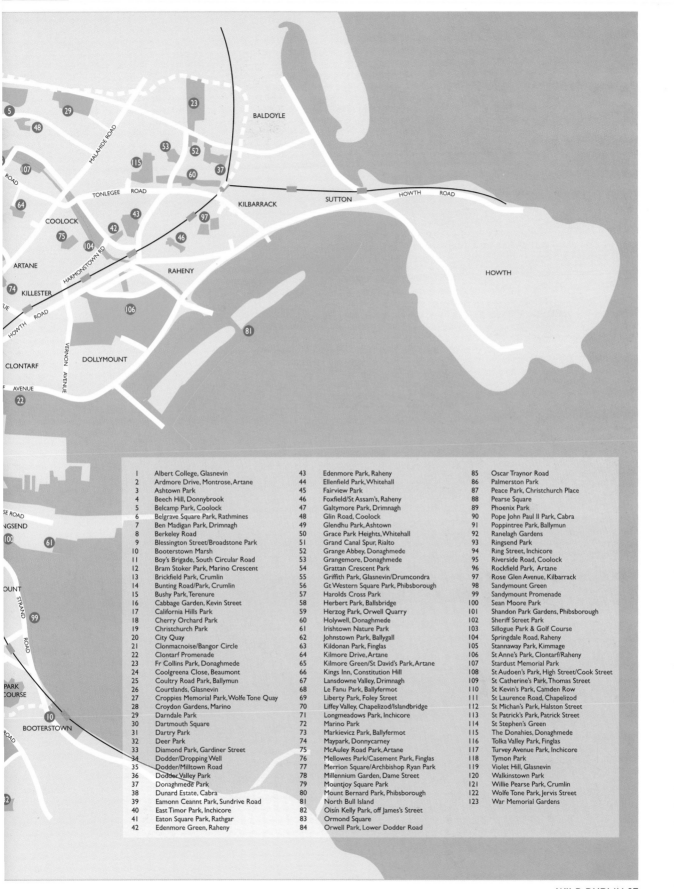

1	Albert College, Glasnevin	43	Edenmore Park, Raheny	85	Oscar Traynor Road
2	Ardmore Drive, Montrose, Artane	44	Ellenfield Park, Whitehall	86	Palmerston Park
3	Ashtown Park	45	Fairview Park	87	Peace Park, Christchurch Place
4	Beech Hill, Donnybrook	46	Foxfield/St Assam's, Raheny	88	Pearse Square
5	Belcamp Park, Coolock	47	Galtymore Park, Drimnagh	89	Pearse Square
6	Belgrave Square Park, Rathmines	48	Glin Road, Coolock	90	Pope John Paul II Park, Cabra
7	Ben Madigan Park, Drimnagh	49	Glendhu Park, Ashtown	91	Poppintree Park, Ballymun
8	Berkeley Road	50	Grace Park Heights, Whitehall	92	Ranelagh Gardens
9	Blessington Street/Broadstone Park	51	Grand Canal Spur, Rialto	93	Ringsend Park
10	Booterstown Marsh	52	Grange Abbey, Donaghmede	94	Ring Street, Inchicore
11	Boy's Brigade, South Circular Road	53	Grangemore, Donaghmede	95	Riverside Road, Coolock
12	Bram Stoker Park, Marino Crescent	54	Grattan Crescent Park	96	Rockfield Park, Artane
13	Brickfield Park, Crumlin	55	Griffith Park, Glasnevin/Drumcondra	97	Rose Glen Avenue, Kilbarrack
14	Bunting Road/Park, Crumlin	56	Gt Western Square Park, Phibsborough	98	Sandymount Green
15	Bushy Park, Terenure	57	Harolds Cross Park	99	Sandymount Promenade
16	Cabbage Garden, Kevin Street	58	Herbert Park, Ballsbridge	100	Sean Moore Park
17	California Hills Park	59	Herzog Park, Orwell Quarry	101	Shandon Park Gardens, Phibsborough
18	Cherry Orchard Park	60	Holywell, Donaghmede	102	Sheriff Street Park
19	Christchurch Park	61	Irishtown Nature Park	103	Sillogue Park & Golf Course
20	City Quay	62	Johnstown Park, Ballygall	104	Springdale Road, Raheny
21	Clonmacnoise/Bangor Circle	63	Kildonan Park, Finglas	105	Stannaway Park, Kimmage
22	Clontarf Promenade	64	Kilmore Drive, Artane	106	St Anne's Park, Clontarf/Raheny
23	Fr Collins Park, Donaghmede	65	Kilmore Green/St David's Park, Artane	107	Stardust Memorial Park
24	Coolgreena Close, Beaumont	66	Kings Inn, Constitution Hill	108	St Audoen's Park, High Street/Cook Street
25	Coultry Road Park, Ballymun	67	Lansdowne Valley, Drimnagh	109	St Catherine's Park, Thomas Street
26	Courtlands, Glasnevin	68	Le Fanu Park, Ballyfermot	110	St Kevin's Park, Camden Row
27	Croppies Memorial Park, Wolfe Tone Quay	69	Liberty Park, Foley Street	111	St Laurence Road, Chapelizod
28	Croydon Gardens, Marino	70	Liffey Valley, Chapelizod/Islandbridge	112	St Michan's Park, Halston Street
29	Darndale Park	71	Longmeadows Park, Inchicore	113	St Patrick's Park, Patrick Street
30	Dartmouth Square	72	Marino Park	114	St Stephen's Green
31	Dartry Park	73	Markievicz Park, Ballyfermot	115	The Donahies, Donaghmede
32	Deer Park	74	Maypark, Donnycarney	116	Tolka Valley Park, Finglas
33	Diamond Park, Gardiner Street	75	McAuley Road Park, Artane	117	Turvey Avenue Park, Inchicore
34	Dodder/Dropping Well	76	Mellowes Park/Casement Park, Finglas	118	Tymon Park
35	Dodder/Milltown Road	77	Merrion Square/Archbishop Ryan Park	119	Violet Hill, Glasnevin
36	Dodder Valley Park	78	Millennium Garden, Dame Street	120	Walkinstown Park
37	Donaghmede Park	79	Mountjoy Square Park	121	Willie Pearse Park, Crumlin
38	Dunard Estate, Cabra	80	Mount Bernard Park, Phibsborough	122	Wolfe Tone Park, Jervis Street
39	Eamonn Ceannt Park, Sundrive Road	81	North Bull Island	123	War Memorial Gardens
40	East Timor Park, Inchicore	82	Oisin Kelly Park, off James's Street		
41	Eaton Square Park, Rathgar	83	Ormond Square		
42	Edenmore Green, Raheny	84	Orwell Park, Lower Dodder Road		

It was really the Georgians and early Victorians who first laid out houses with gardens and open squares in the 1700s-1800s. The Edwardians put red-brick houses in our suburbs, with front and back gardens and more squares and parks, at the beginning of the 1900s. Semi-detached Dublin was built in the second half of the twentieth century. Low density housing with garages and gardens, greens and play areas, were a feature of this era. Now in the early twenty-first century we are back to high density dwelling again – this time in apartment blocks of higher and higher size, almost approaching skyscraper level in places. Never were our greens, parks and gardens more necessary – both for ourselves and for wildlife.

Many of our larger parks and gardens in Dublin City are managed by Dublin City Council. Such parks include Tolka Valley Park, Poppintree Park, St Anne's Park, Fairview Park and Mountjoy Square. On the south side of the Liffey are Irishtown Nature Park, Ringsend Park, Sean Moore Park, Herbert Park, Ranelagh Gardens, St Stephen's Green, Iveagh Gardens, Merrion Square, Harolds Cross Park, Deer Park, Eamonn Ceannt Park, Brickfields Park, Walkinstown Park and Bushy Park.

The Dublin City habitat mapping project, completed in 2007, estimated that at least 45% of the city is not built on. The green spaces in the city make up to 25%, with public parks, graveyards and green spaces, while private gardens account for another 20% of the ground area. No wonder there is such a variety of wildlife in our urban area.

This page: Lake in the Phoenix Park
Opposite left: Dartmouth Square

MAMMALS

The following pages describe the wildlife that live in Dublin's parks, gardens, and can even be found in the city's graveyards. Ireland is home to thirty-two species of land mammals including ten species of bats. Of these twenty-four live in Dublin City, many of them in our city gardens.

HEDGEHOGS

One of the most loved garden creatures is the hedgehog – everyone wants one in their garden. Hedgehogs eat snails and slugs, caterpillars, beetles, earthworms and millipedes – this much loved creature is a carnivore. The first time a garden owner becomes aware that a hedgehog has taken up residence in the garden is when the family dog is heard protesting loudly because a trespassing hedgehog is gobbling up the food in his bowl. But hedgehogs are not territorial; when they have hoovered up all the available slugs and snails they will move on, climbing over walls if necessary. They spend the winter in hibernation – a mound of leaves under the garden shed can be very suitable for this activity.

PYGMY SHREW

The other insectivore that frequents the gardens and parks of Dublin is our smallest mammal – the Pygmy shrew. It is difficult to find, however, as it is so small – most sightings are by accident. One ran over this author's shoe one afternoon in Leinster Road in Rathmines and was none the worse for the experience as it scuttled away into the undergrowth. They are most usually seen as offerings brought in by the family cat.

• •
Hedgehog, urban back garden

FIELD MOUSE

The cat might also bring in other offerings from the garden: a young rat, a House mouse or the endearing little Field mouse. This creature, which normally inhabits hedgerows, can sometimes come into houses in the winter time. The Field mouse differs from the House mouse in having larger eyes and ears. It is also known for its habit of leaping into the air when startled.

Because shrews eat things like woodlice, flies, earwigs, spiders and beetles their flesh is smelly and does not appeal to cats that, while they will kill them, won't eat them. Shrews are really very tiny – about half the size of a Field mouse – and they must eat almost continually to keep up their high metabolic rate. So eating like a Pygmy shrew means eating your own weight in food every day – surely no compliment when said to a human!

Pygmy shrew, Phoenix Park

BATS

Of our ten Irish bat species, eight occur in our city area. Bats are nocturnal mammals that scour our night skies searching for moths, midges and mosquitoes on which to feed during the summer. They emerge from their hibernation roosts in attics of old buildings and in crevices and hollows of old mature trees in late March/early April and the females move into attic spaces, belfries and cracks and crevices in old walls and bridges. These are their summer roosts or maternity quarters and it is here that they will give birth to their young – one each. Young bats are reared exclusively by their mothers, who feed them on milk when they return from their foraging flights. Babies are fully weaned by the end of the summer and practise feeding and flying before the whole lot go back into their hibernation roosts by Halloween. Some species can live up to twenty years.

Needless to say, bats are not blind and they do not fly into people's hair, so there is absolutely no need to be afraid of them. Bats emit ultrasonic sounds and are able to detect where they are going by bouncing these sounds off objects all around them. Each species emits these sounds at a different pitch, so by using a bat detector, which detects and records the pitch being emitted, it is possible to tell what species of bat is flying overhead. Dublin has a very active bat group, which has recorded Dublin's bats over the last few years. Bats are highly protected by Irish and European law, and identified as priority species in the DCC, Biodiversity Action Plan. City centre parks such as St Stephen's Green, Blessington Street Basin – both of which have ponds – the Grand and Royal Canals, and Merrion Square, which is fringed with trees, are particularly important for bats, as are suburban parks such as Marlay Park, Bushy Park, St Anne's Park and the Phoenix Park.

Long-eared bat

Common pipistrelle bat

The following bat species occur in the Dublin City area:

DAUBENTON'S BAT

This bat feeds mainly on insects over water, such as midges, caddis flies and mosquitoes. It can be found flying over the Grand and Royal Canals, and over the lake in Marlay Park.

LEISLER'S BAT is our largest Irish bat species. It generally feeds over fields and parklands. It feeds on moths and beetles. There is a summer roost in St Enda's Park and it has been recorded flying over Blessington Street Basin, the Grand Canal from Mount Street to Ranelagh Bridge, and in St Stephen's Green.

WHISKERED BAT

This is considered to be one of our rarest bat species. There is an old record for this species from the grounds of St Patrick's College in Drumcondra. More recently it was detected flying over St Stephen's Green in the city centre.

LONG-EARED BAT

This is the easiest bat to record in the hand because of its very long ears and is often recorded by bird ringers as it swoops into their mist nets in search of moths. It is also able to pick its food off vegetation so such creatures as spiders, beetles and earwigs feature in its diet. It has been recorded in Bushy Park and in Marlay Park.

PIPISTRELLE

There are three species of pipistrelle bat on the Irish List now, the Common, Soprano and Nathusius – all of which are found in the Dublin area. The Nathusius was found recently in the Phoenix Park.

The **Common pipistrelle** is probably the most abundant bat in Europe. It is our second smallest bat – only the other Dublin pipistrelle, the Soprano pipistrelle, is smaller. Its adult body weight in summer is a mere five grammes but it is still able to eat up to 3,000 midges in a night, not to mention lots of mosquitoes as well. Humans – who are not too fond of midges and mosquitoes – should encourage bats in their area by planting trees and shrubs in their gardens to make the bats feel at home.

The **Soprano pipistrelle** species has only recently been distinguished from the Common pipistrelle by virtue of its higher call as recorded on the bat detector. It emits hunting calls at 55 Kilohertz as opposed to the Common pipistrelle whose hunting calls are emitted at 45 Kilohertz. It is also slightly smaller than the Common pipistrelle, being up to 2 grammes lighter. It has been detected flying over St Stephen's Green and over Glasnevin Cemetery.

SQUIRRELS – RED AND GREY

An abundance of squirrels live in our city parks, and indeed are frequent visitors to our back gardens. It is easy to see them scampering along the ground or whisking up the trunks of trees. Fine sunny days in winter are very good for observing them as the low sunlight illuminates them. Squirrels of course do not hibernate. They spend all September gathering and storing food for winter because they will need it when food is hard to find. They stay indoors in their untidy nest of sticks, known as a drey, when the day is cold and wet and tuck into their stores. And on bright days they are out and about and are easy to see.

RED SQUIRREL

In 2008 there are Red squirrels left only in the following places: St Anne's Park and on Dalkey and Killiney Hills. The Red squirrel is a smaller, daintier species that feeds on pine cones, hazelnuts and very ripe acorns. Its feeding habits are more environmentally harmonious than Grey squirrels, as they do not damage trees to the same extent, because they are not so dependent on

NATTERER'S BAT

There is an old post-1950 record for this bat species from Ballybrack. Its summer roosts are usually found in cracks and crevices in stone archways or between rafters in roofs, so they are difficult to detect. They feed around trees and in woodland canopy and, as well as catching moths, can hover over prey and scoop it up with their tail. They can also land on the ground and catch earwigs and centipedes.

Red squirrel in St Anne's Park

bark and buds for food. The unwanted arrival of the Grey squirrel in Dublin has caused great damage to the trees in the Phoenix Park. A widespread planting of trees was carried out there fifteen years ago and the trees there are now big enough to support the weight of the Grey squirrel as it climbs out to the end of the branches to nibble the bark and destroy the buds and growing points.

GREY SQUIRREL

The squirrel that is commonly seen all over Dublin City is the larger grey squirrel. This brash creature is a native of North America and was introduced to Ireland in 1911. A basket of six grey ____ were given as a present at a wedding of ____ in Castleforbes in County ____ ned the squirrels leapt ____ ing woodlands. ____ since then, ____ nirty years ago. They have ____ e native red squirrel wherever they have spread. There ____ sons for this. They eat a more varied diet ____ the red and are able to digest unripe acorns – thus eating the red squirrels out of house and home, as it were. The red squirrel can only eat ripe acorns, and when there are grey squirrels in their area they eat all the acorns before they ripen sufficiently for the red to digest. ____ are also several squirrel diseases asso____ grey to which they are immune but ____ can spread to the red, who have no defenc____ them.

Grey squirrel in the
Botanic Gardens

Fallow deer bucks, Phoenix Park

FALLOW DEER

Another introduction to the Phoenix Park is the Fallow deer. These deer were brought to Ireland by the Normans as a source of food – and deer parks were established for them in various parts of the country. The Phoenix Park was one such, and deer have been kept here since the seventeenth century. Male fallow deer – the bucks – have flat palmate antlers, while the female does and the young fawns have none. Rutting takes place in September, when the bucks fight fiercely for the favours of the ladies, who look on apparently without much interest. However, the most successful buck is able to operate a harem system, so the winner takes all. Fawns are born in June in the areas of long grass in the park and will lie quite still for a day or so while their mother makes careful visits to feed them. The deer in the park are studied by the Zoology Department of UCD, and the numbers are managed so that the park doesn't exceed its carrying capacity of about 450 deer.

In a normal wildlife situation there would be wolves in the ecosystem to keep deer numbers at a manageable level. There are, however, no wolves in Ireland since 1786, when the last one was shot in Carlow, so herd management is necessary to ensure that the motor car doesn't inadvertently assume the role of the wolf, killing deer that might wander on to the main roads in the park at night because of pressure of numbers. Newborn fawns are counted and tagged each June and surplus ones are removed and reared away from the park.

The other two species of Irish deer – the Sika and the Red – do not occur in Dublin. Sika are common in Wicklow, while Red deer – our only native species – occur in Killarney National Park in Kerry. A small amount of deer are also farmed in Ireland and are sold as venison.

Fallow deer fawn, Phoenix Park

BADGERS

Badgers are surprisingly common in the city – not only in suburban gardens, but right in the centre of the city too. One bemused Dubliner resolved to go out at night no more when he met a badger walking along the pavement in Lower Baggot Street at 2.00am. This late-night reveller was not looking for a winebar, but for a discarded hamburger or chips, as badgers are scavengers as well as enthusiastic eaters of earthworms, berries, slugs, rats and mice. This one had been using the canal as a wildlife corridor to walk though the sleeping city. The Tolka, the Royal Canal, and the River Dodder are haunts for them too and they have setts in the more inaccessible parts of these areas. They were greatly discommoded when the disused Harcourt Street railway line turned into the Luas; evicted and dispossessed badgers took up residence in Airfield and larger back gardens nearby. Most of Dublin's larger parks are home to badgers, as are the larger graveyards and back gardens in newer housing estates, which were built on traditional badger territory. The M50 is an effective barrier in keeping 'culchie' badgers away from the city ones as there are no underpasses to allow visits.

Badgers in a garden in Rathfarnham

FOXES

While foxes roam the streets of Dublin by night they are also common in back gardens, where kind-hearted Dubliners are likely to feed them. They have their dens in overgrown gardens or in the less used parts of parks and hospital grounds. They are partial to golf courses, where a sighting can provide an uplifting moment for a golfer searching for a lost ball.

While they mainly confine their wanderings to nocturnal forays, in late autumn they can be seen in broad daylight out and about in search of food. These are the cubs – mostly male – who were born the previous June and are now being turned out of their homes by their parents, who hold the territory and wish to breed again. Young females are allowed to stay in the territory as they can help with the rearing of next year's cubs. The young inexperienced male foxes can find it difficult to find territory for themselves and often don't survive into the next year. Dublin City is probably at its capacity for foxes. The advent of the wheelie bin doesn't seem to have had the feared reduction of its numbers, as some opposers of this method of waste collection once feared.

STOAT

This secretive carnivore is very difficult to spot but it has been recorded in Glasnevin Cemetery. This quite ferocious animal can kill rabbits, which are much larger than itself, by apparently hypnotising them through staring at them as it performs a type of dancing movement. It then suddenly pounces on the rabbit, killing it with a bite to the jugular vein. It also eats birds' eggs, nestlings, mice, rats – in short any creature it can nab. It has even been recorded scavenging along the shoreline in Dalkey. Stoats are relatively common in rural areas where there are stone walls for them to nest in. There are no weasels in Ireland – this creature, which is smaller than the stoat, is native in Britain, but it never colonised Ireland after the last Ice Age.

CREEPY-CRAWLIES AND GARDEN WILDLIFE

While the invertebrate fauna of back gardens can be classified according to officially approved scientific phyla and families, there is really only one way to consider them: whether they are liked or disliked by householders and gardeners.

LADYBIRDS

Ladybirds are a favourite with most gardeners. As well as looking attractive, they are also good at removing unwanted pests in the garden. These are carnivorous beetles that hunt during the day and feed on aphids, such as greenflies and whiteflies, which are not on any gardener's popular list. They don't bite humans, but will excrete a warning coloured liquid if held too long in the hand. There are eighteen Irish recorded species, many of which occur in the city. One that is particularly associated with the warmer urban areas is the Two-spot ladybird *Adalia bipunctata*. This is a small red ladybird with one black spot on each wing case, known as elytra. The Seven-spot ladybird *Coccinella 7-punctata* is a much larger species with three black spots on each wing case and one spot in the middle. The presence of both together in city gardens has probably given rise to the myth that you can tell a ladybird's age by the number of spots it has. Though the Seven-spot ladybird is bigger than the Two-spot, in fact they are different types of ladybirds – one did not grow into the other, acquiring more spots in the process.

There are also yellow ladybirds – the Fourteen-spot *Propylea 14-punctata*, and the Twenty-two spot *Psyllobora 22-punctata,* all of which sport the appropriate number of black spots on a yellow background. Indeed some of our ladybirds have cream spots, such as the Eighteen-spot *Myrrha 18-guttata*, the cream spot *Calvia 14-guttata* and the orange ladybird *Halyzia 16-guttata*. All these ladybirds live in hedges, gardens and wooded areas and are most active between April and September. But one thing does not vary – they are all poisonous to any bird that might venture to gobble one. Their bodies contain a pungent acid and many of them will exude a coloured liquid, to warn that they should not be eaten. Their bright colours are a warning to would-be predators, so they don't need to hide.

Bumble bee and Seven-spot ladybird
Inset: Two-spot ladybird

BEES

Other insects with bright warning colours are bees. These also rank among our favourite insects and Dublin's gardens and parks resound with the hum of busy bees on a sunny summer's day.

BUMBLE BEES

Our native wild bees are the Bumble bees – the big furry bees that first appear out of hibernation on a sunny March day and convince us all that spring has returned. These are social insects; there is a queen that lays all the eggs, and worker bees that forage our garden flowers for pollen and nectar to bring back to the nest. Nests are small affairs built in abandoned mouse holes in the ground and they are built anew each year, as only the new queens, born at the end of the summer, will hibernate after their marriage flight. The most commonly seen species are the Red-tailed bumble bee *Bombus lapidarius*, the large White-tailed bumble bee *Bombus lucorum* – queens are very obvious in gardens in early spring – and the Common carder bee *Bombus pascuorum* – the bee with the orange shoulders, as it were. Bumble bee workers are all very loyal to their queens, and like any social insect, will sting if they feel their nest is under threat, but they are quite laid back and there are rarely reports of persons being stung by Bumble bees.

MINING BEES

In many suburban gardens, particularly across the south of Dublin City where the soil is well worked and sandy, householders notice that the bees in their garden are silent and fly in and out of holes in the ground. What they are observing are Mining bees *Andrena fulva*, a species of solitary bee. These bees are not social insects, like Honey bees and wasps. Each female is fully developed and digs a hole in sandy soil in which she lays an egg. The bees all live close together – a Mining bee housing estate, as it were – but because each one has an independent home there is no queen, and therefore the bees have no defensive sting and they do not hum or communicate with each other.

Each bee excavates a tunnel in the ground in the month of May and lays an egg at the end of it. It is then stocked with pollen and nectar, which the female collects from nearby flowers and deposits in the burrow during frequent visits. She will be dead before her progeny emerges later on in the year. This newly emerged Mining bee will visit flowers, mate and then hibernate and continue the cycle the following year. In May when the females are excavating tunnels, laying eggs and provisioning the new baby, there will be a lot of focused activity in the garden, which is sometimes disconcerting to the garden owner. Male Mining bees do no housekeeping chores – they just mate with the females and leave all the work to them. These bees are quite harmless and play an important role in the pollination of garden plants.

Mining bee

HONEY BEES

On any herbaceous border in a city park Bumble bees are more common than Honey bees, as bee keepers do not generally keep working hives in built-up urban areas. But we do see Honey bees there and these are probably Honey bees that have swarmed from hives and flown off to build their own colonies in the wild. Honey bees *Apis mellifera* are natives of South East Asia and were brought to Ireland by monks in early Christian times as a source of honey. They do not hibernate, the queen can live for up to three years and the reason they make so much honey is to tide them over the winter when there are no flowers and it's too cold to go out and forage. New queens return to the old nest (it is the old queen who leaves with a swarm of her cronies when the nest becomes overcrowded) so a bee's nest can last for many years and grow to quite enormous sizes.

Wasp collecting material for nest

WASPS

This is not the case with the wasp's nest. It is made of paper made by the wasps from chewed wood and while it can be as large as a football by October, it is not retained from one year to the next. Like bumble bees, wasps are natives and only the new queen born and mated at the end of August will hibernate; all the rest will die off as winter approaches. Wasps are a particularly useful species to have in a garden as they are carnivores and they collect vast numbers of small insects such as aphids to feed the growing larvae in the nest. The adult wasps, who have a sweet tooth, can satisfy it at home by licking up the sweet dribble the contented well-fed larvae produce. Each generation lives for six weeks, spending all its time feeding the next generation with garden insect pests. This sustainable arrangement only breaks down at the end of August when the old queen dies of exhaustion having laid up to 40,000 eggs. The youngest crop of wasps have no larvae to feed and consequently no supply of sweet liquid at home. It is this last generation of wasps that becomes a pest to us in its search for sugar and gives all wasps a bad name. The Common wasp *Vespula vulgaris* is the one most usually seen.

HOVERFLY

But every black and yellow striped flying insect is not a bee or a wasp with a deadly sting. There are several inhabitants of urban gardens who don these colours in order to fool their mortal enemies the birds, who fear, with justification, a mouthful of bee or wasp complete with sting. Hoverflies are two-winged creatures with large eyes who visit colourful flowers to feed on nectar. They can beat their wings so fast that they can hover in the air in front of flowers and indeed can fly backwards. They feed their offspring on aphids. They have no sting and so are very welcome creatures in the gardens of those who recognise them for what they are. At least four different species visit Dublin's gardens and parks.

Hoverfly

Wasp's nest

WOOD WASP

There is another stripy flying insect that puts the fear of God into many people who feel that it must be a hornet, as it has what appears to be a huge sting sticking out of its nether regions. We have no hornet species at all in this country – so far they have only made it as far as the south of England. What is being viewed with such horror is a Wood wasp *Urocerus gigas,* a member of the sawfly family. This insect has an ovipositor at its rear end, not a sting, which consists of a long saw to enable it to drill a hole in timber in order to lay its egg deep in the timber. This species lays its eggs in conifer trees, but as it takes up to three years for it to develop into an adult, the timber is often part of a new house before the creature emerges, terrifying the new home owner. Adults are on the wing between June and October and make a loud buzzing noise as they fly.

GARDEN ANT

The ant that takes to the skies in huge flying mating colonies over our city's streets is the adult version of another very common garden resident – the Garden ant. This is a perfectly normal inhabitant of light-sandy coastal soils, where a colony will set up a nest, which will contain one or more egg-laying queens and hundreds, or even thousands, of wingless workers. They have a fondness for honeydew – the sweet liquid excreted by greenflies – and often seem to be 'milking' them, stroking them as it were, to make the aphids release the sweet liquid from their posterior regions. They seem to guard the aphids from raids by hungry ladybirds. As more and more city inhabitants dig up their gardens and replace the soil with patio slabs laid on a bed of sand, the more suitable habitats are being created for this Black garden ant *Lasius niger*. And they use the gardens, and indeed indoors in houses to forage for food. But at least this species has no sting.

Garden ants about to take flight

Meadow brown

BUTTERFLIES

There are twenty-two species of butterfly recorded in Dublin City. The coastal ones are discussed in chapter four covering that area. Our gardens and parks have their own typical species, some of which are more welcome than others. Gardens where vegetables, such as cabbage and rocket, are grown and which have nasturtium flowers in the borders will be beloved of members of the White butterfly family, who lay their eggs on these food plants. The Large, Small and Green-veined white butterflies all come from voracious caterpillars that have dined ravenously on these plants.

Garden hedges support the Speckled wood butterfly and the Dark-green fritillary, while the grasses in our urban parks are the food plants of the Wall brown and the Meadow brown. Nettles and docks feed the caterpillars of the Small copper, the Peacock, and indeed the Small tortoiseshell. All these caterpillars become furry or shiny as they get bigger and finally pupate into adult butterflies, well away from the food plant.

Green-veined white

Convolvulus hawkmoth

MOTHS

Most moths fly at night and come to lighted windows during summer nights. There are many more species of moth than butterfly in Ireland – there are upwards of two thousand on the Irish List. Many of them have dull brown forewings but the back wings can be brightly coloured in red or yellow. These are usually kept hidden under the forewings while the moth is at rest. However, if the moth is attacked, it quickly opens its wings and a flash of these vivid underwings can startle a predator and give the moth time to escape; species such as the Garden tiger and the Large yellow underwing come into this category.

The largest moths belong to the Hawkmoth family. These have enormous caterpillars with a horn at one end, which are quite often noticed by gardeners, but the adults themselves are usually even more spectacular. The Death's head hawkmoth sports a skull and crossbones on its back, the Elephant hawkmoth is bright pink in colour, the Convolvulus hawkmoth has vivid pink stripes on its body and the Hummingbird hawkmoth flies during the day and hovers in front of flowers like a miniature humming bird.

SNAILS

Many garden creepy crawlies are unpopular with gardeners. Top of this list must be the Mollusc family – the slugs and snails. These are all hermaphrodites which means that each individual has both male and female parts, and while it needs another individual to mate with, it means that each one will lay up to 100 eggs in the garden soil, thus ensuring the survival of the next generation. Because slugs and snails are moist soft-bodied creatures they are nocturnal, coming out when it is cool and moist to feed on plants with their rasping tongues and then slipping away to hide in a sheltered spot, such as under flowerpots, window sills, behind large leaves and under debris and stones, in sheltered parts of trees – anywhere they won't dry out during the day time. Sometimes during very dry summers they will congregate in large numbers on the shady side of trees to avoid drying out.

An escargatoire of snails on the shady side of a tree

Two garden snails entwined

There are several varieties of snails to be found in Dublin's gardens and parks. The most easily seen and recognised is the Garden snail *Helix aspera* – a large creature with a shell length of up to 40mm. It is very fond of the green leaves of our favourite garden plants and will also eat newly-planted seedlings. It can congregate in large numbers on the underside of tree branches to sit out any spells of summer dry weather. The Srawberry snail *Trichia striolata*, as its name indicates, specialises in making holes in ripe strawberries but it is quite partial to lettuce as well. The White lipped and Brown lipped snails *Cepaea hortensis* and *C. nemoralis* add a bit of colour to the scene as their shells have a yellowish base colour adorned with spiral stripes of black, white, brown, grey and beige. These prefer garden plants too, but can eat grass if they are desperate.

SLUGS

Slugs have an even worse reputation among gardeners than snails do. There are several particularly voracious species that are common and widespread in Dublin City. The Common garden slug *Arion distinctus* will eat almost any garden plant above or below the ground and can do serious damage to potato tubers. It leaves an orange mucus trail. The Netted slug *Deroceras reticulatum* which is beige-brown in colour is another major garden pest. It hides away during the day right inside the cabbages and lettuces it has been dining on during the night. The Large black slug *Arion ater* eats carrion, dung and rotting vegetation. It occurs in an orange form as well and contracts to a quivering blob if disturbed. This one, however, does a great deal of good, despite its unprepossessing appearance. It is quite often found in compost bins, where it lays clusters of pearly-white round eggs after helping with the recycling of the organic matter therein.

Netted slugs

Centipede on stone

Centipedes and **Black ground beetles** are carnivores that use Dublin's parks and gardens as hunting grounds at night. Beauty is in the eye of the beholder and to greet these creatures with cries of disgust surely betrays the arrogance of the human observers. Both of these types of creatures are fast running nocturnal predators that catch and kill slugs, earwigs and the like. The Devil's coach-horse is

Millipede on leaf

Devil's coach-horse on leaf

a particularly long black ground beetle. It will stand and cock up its tail at any would-be attacker including humans, and, like the centipede, is capable of giving a handler a nip. **Millipedes**, on the other hand, are slow moving invertebrates with two pairs of legs on each segment (which may add up to several hundred – but never a thousand, despite its name). These are all herbivorous species, that feed on dead plant matter and so are part of the recycling army that every park and garden needs. Looks don't come into it!

Dublin's graveyards

There are at least eighty-six graveyards in the Dublin City Council area alone and many others in the different areas covered in this book. The Dublin City graveyards have been studied for both their natural history and their cultural heritage (Wilson F, Goodbody R and Nairn R, *Dublin City Graveyards Study – a report for Dublin City Council*, 2004). This report outlines in detail the wide biodiversity in Dublin's graveyards – particularly in the old graveyards that are no longer in use. Fifteen of Dublin's mammals have been recorded there, twenty-six different species of birds, ten species of butterflies, forty-eight species of trees – nineteen of which are native – and over a hundred herbaceous plants which are established in the wild. None of these, however, are just confined to graveyards – they can be found too in the parks and gardens nearby, although the graveyards play a very important part in providing habitat for the biodiversity of wildlife in Dublin City.

PROTESTANT WOODLICE

There is however a species of invertebrate that is not only confined to graveyards, but to Protestant graveyards at that. This is the species of woodlouse known as *Androniscus dentiger*, a small pale-coloured woodlouse that has no common English name. This creature lives under paving stones and slabs and beneath gravel on paths where conditions are moist. It has a special affinity with old churchyards, but the peculiar thing is that it seems to be most likely a Protestant churchyard where it is found. Why? Can woodlice distinguish the religion of a graveyard? What seems to be the case is that Protestant graveyards in general tend to be older than Catholic ones. The structures in the oldest parts of these have ox blood mortar in the walls and it is on this that these particular woodlice feed.

There are several other common species of woodlice found in all graveyards – the Pill woodlouse *Armadillidium vulgare*, which rolls into a ball if disturbed, the Common woodlouse *Oniscus asellus* and another darker one *Porcellio scaber*. These are all experts on recycling dead leaf litter and rotten wood. In fact, of the twenty-eight species of woodlice recorded in Ireland, twenty have been recorded as occurring in Dublin within the boundary of the M50 wherever they can find suitable habitat.

Porcellio scaber

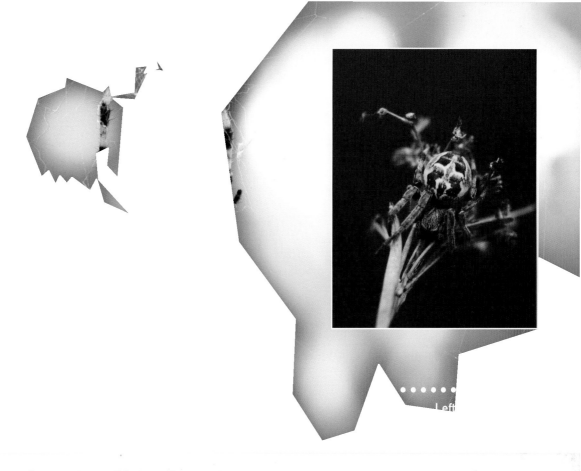

Left

No account of invertebrate life in urban parks and gardens would be complete without a mention of spiders. All spiders are carnivorous cannibals and Dublin's spiders are no exception. Luckily all of our native species are too small to inflict injury on humans but they certainly make short work of any creature their own size – even their own species – as many a hapless male setting forth to mate has discovered. There are hundreds of Irish species, very many of which reside in the parks, gardens and even houses of Dublin's citizenry.

In autumn every year the web-spinning spiders are very obvious. One such is the Garden spider *Araneus diadematus* distinguished by its black and yellow stripy legs and by the white cross on its brown pea-sized back. This spider spins a wheel-like orb web on the outside of windows. There are about forty web-spinning spiders and they make webs particular in design to each species. The biggest spiders, however, are the Hunting spiders. These run around at night sinking their fangs into such prey as woodlice, earwigs, flies, aphids, moths, indeed anything they can creep up on. Spiders such as the Zebra spider *Salticus scenicus* and the Wolf spider *Pardosa amentata* are among this lot. One species of spider, the Crab spider *Misumena vatia* lurks in white or yellow flowers and adopts the colour of that flower. So when an unsuspecting bee or fly or butterfly lands on the flower for a feed of nectar this camouflaged assassin grabs it, biting it quickly behind the head and thus securing its meal – fast food delivery as it were!

Spiders live in houses too. The so-called Bath spider *Tegenaria gigantea* is one of the largest spiders in Europe. The females can have a body size up to 16mm long and when you consider that the legs can be three times the length of this, it is fairly large when spotted trapped in the bath. A thin spider with immensely long legs hangs upside down from the corner of the ceiling of most city houses and vibrates itself into a blur when touched. This is *Pholcus phalangioides* which used to be called the Cellar spider but now, as it is very abundant in centrally heated houses, is called the Daddy-long-legs spider. This of course has nothing to do with the winged insect with six long legs – the Crane fly – which is the original Daddy-long-legs that flies into houses in August attracted by the lights.

All spiders do immense amounts of good in gardens, feeding on pests such as aphids and flies.

CITY BIRDS

Two hundred and fourteen species of birds have been recorded in Dublin City. Almost half of these are garden birds, many of which are beloved of householders whose gardens they inhabit. Birdwatch Ireland have been conducting a survey of garden birds over the last number of years and have drawn up a list of the twenty most widespread species found in back gardens. They have also counted the numbers of individuals found

Hooded crow in flight

and the results are fascinating to anyone interested in birds.

Amazingly, in 99% of city gardens, the robin, the blackbird and the Blue tit can be seen at some stage of the year. Robins are practically tame and the presence of someone working in the garden lures it in to find the insects that have been disturbed by the activity. Blackbirds are really common in Dublin and their alarm call can be commonly heard particularly in early evening. The Blue tit and its larger relative the Great tit (which has been recorded in 90% of gardens surveyed), are very acrobatic birds commonly seen on bird feeders. They nest in holes in trees and can be encouraged to nest with the provision of nest boxes with appropriately-sized entrance holes. Blue tits in particular pick unusual places to nest – one pair chose the traffic lights in St Stephen's Green and seemed completely unfazed by the sounds and colours as they changed (and indeed by the queues of traffic waiting impatiently). In 2007 it was a set of lights near Glasnevin Cemetery that provided the nest site. June is the month to keep an eye out for such activity – gridlock will turn us all into expert bird watchers!

CROW FAMILY

Crows are very common in our back gardens and indeed in our city parks and playing pitches. Magpies, rooks and jackdaws are the most commonly seen of our seven Irish crow species.

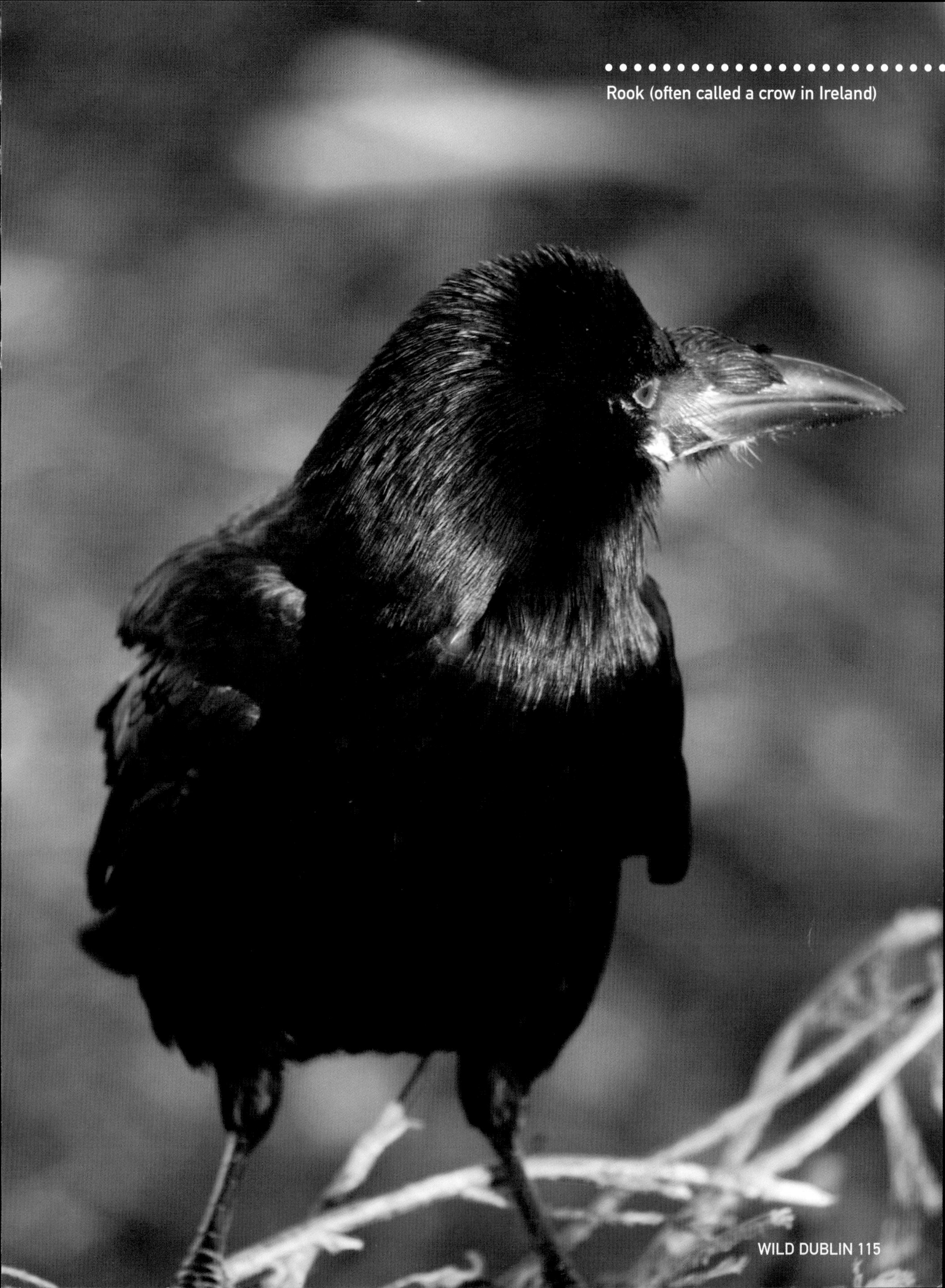

Rook (often called a crow in Ireland)

Magpies seem to be the bane of householders' lives – they can occur in gangs of up to seven or eight. Magpies nest at the tops of tall trees and launch marauding attacks on the cat's bowl, the cat itself, the nests of small birds and, heartbreakingly, baby birds when they are learning to fly in summer. Magpies are very clever birds and have really adapted extremely well to living in suburbia. They also eat snails, slugs, earthworms, rubbish and indeed used to copy the blue tits and drink milk out of the tops of milk bottles on doorsteps until the whole practice of delivering milk in bottles was discontinued fifteen years ago. There are eight magpies' nests in the trees along Eglinton Road. Magpies can even build nests on street lamps, if there is pressure on building space. Though it has never been proved that magpies steal shiny valuable objects and hide them in their nests, one enterprising pair of magpies built a nest entirely out of wire coat hangers on the balcony of 35 Parnell Square – the headquarters of the Irish National Teachers' Organisation. The pair successfully reared three young.

Jackdaws are chimney nesters and there is no shortage of chimneys in the city where they can try their luck. Together with the **rooks** (commonly called crows in Dublin) they forage on playing pitches, lawns and grassy parks for leatherjackets (which are the young of the Daddy-long-legs Crane fly), cockchafers (the larvae of the maybugs), earthworms and fly larvae of all sorts, which form a large part of their diet. Rooks nest in rookeries high up in the trees in the Phoenix Park, St Anne's Park and Bushy Park.

Jackdaw on Wellington monument

Magpie

Hooded crows

The **Hooded crow** – that nasty mean-looking scavenger so detested by hill farmers because of the harm they do to sheep, pecking out their eyes and blinding them – occasionally makes an appearance and is easily recognised by its black head and its grey shoulders. More often seen in moors and mountains, the **raven**, the largest member of the crow species, can be spotted by eagle-eyed observers in Irishtown Park as it forages for carrion. A raven was also spotted in early December 2007 flying over the grounds of Terenure College. The **jay** is our most colourful crow and can be spotted in several places in Dublin City. It is most readily seen in the Phoenix Park feeding on the ground in early winter. It gathers acorns in autumn and stores them individually as winter supplies. The jay has a phenomenal memory as it can remember where it put them all as it needs them.

Jay – our most colourful crow

BIRDS OF PREY

Birds of prey are the magpies, only real enemy – specifically the sparrowhawk. A huge commotion in a garden in Terenure alerted the owner to the sight of a beady-eyed female sparrowhawk deftly plucking and eating a freshly killed magpie, while being utterly disdainful of the racket caused by its protesting relatives, who were careful to keep a safe distance. Peregrine falcons, kestrels, buzzards and merlins are all recorded as occurring in our city, while the definitive list of city birds also includes rare sightings of such exotic birds of prey as Hen harrier, goshawk, osprey, hobby and Marsh harrier. The Barn owl, the Short-eared owl and the Long-eared owl are also on this list. Short-eared owls are winter migrants that hunt by day over Bull Island, while the Long-eared owl is a woodland resident heard more commonly than seen at night in parks such as the Tolka Valley Park and the Phoenix Park.

Winter brings flocks of visitors from continental Europe to our gardens looking for berries. Blackcaps are seen regularly once winter sets in, as are bramblings – a colourful finch from Northern Europe. Foreign thrush species – mainly fieldfares, although sometimes redwings too – have been recorded as well, scouring hedges for haws and holly berries. The winter visitor that causes the biggest frisson of excitement, however, is the waxwing. A flock of fifteen to twenty were seen at Jury's Hotel/American Embassy, in Ballsbridge in December 2006. These are most exotic looking birds from Scandinavia, as big as starlings, with pink brown heads and a black eye mask. They are quite tame and will sit for a long time on the berried bushes on which they feed.

COMMON GARDEN BIRDS

In fact the availability of food in a garden, whether it is a plentiful selection of slugs, aphids and other insects in summer or berries and well-stocked bird tables in winter, and the absence of a territorial cat will determine the abundance and variety of birds seen by alert householders. The common garden bird list includes chaffinch, greenfinch, goldfinch, siskin, House sparrow, wren, dunnock, Pied wagtail, Coal tit and Collared dove among its top twenty, while Long-tailed tits, treecreepers, bullfinches, goldcrests and linnets can all be spotted too, particularly if the garden backs on to one of Dublin's many city parks.

Chaffinch, city garden

Sparrow feeding, city garden

Wren peeping out of a bird house, city garden

Beech tree displaying magnificent roots, Bushy Park

TREES AND WILDFLOWERS

Dublin is a city that has dramatically expanded in recent years. New housing estates, roads and parks cover areas that were formerly open countryside or parkland surrounding 'big houses'. The trees and wild plants of the city still reflect this former time. Quite often the small front garden of a terraced street will have trees that are patently out of scale with the housing and reflect the planting that was kept when the land was parcelled up for housing. Grosvenor Road in Rathmines boasts fine specimens of Walnut, Arbutus and large Yew trees, all of greater age than the houses in whose gardens they are. The trees in the grounds of what is at the moment still the Berkeley Court Hotel in Ballsbridge were once specimen trees in Trinity College's Botanic gardens. The Strawberry tree there, *Arbutus andrachnoides,* is the second tallest of its kind in Ireland. The Mulberry tree in the grounds of Rathmines Castle – now the grounds of the Church of Ireland Training College – was there at the time of Cromwell in 1649. Tradition has it that he tethered his horse to it when he dropped in for a visit on his way back from sacking Drogheda and killing all its inhabitants. The Box elder *Acer negundo* in a garden in Leeson Park Road in Ranelagh is the second greatest girthed tree of its kind in the country. The Fern-leaf beech *Fagus sylvatica* in the gardens of Mount Anville School in Goatstown at 3.76 x 20 metres is a landmark tree. The biggest Silver maple in Ireland is found in the People's Garden in the Phoenix Park and there is a most amazing specimen of Locust tree in the grounds of the White Fathers in Templeogue.

Hawthorn tree, Phoenix Park

Laburnum in bloom

While enthusiastic gardeners will plant all sorts of shrubs and hedging in their gardens, much of it exotic non-native species, there is an amazing 19.6km of intact hedgerows still left in Dublin City. These are present in public parks, private gardens, schools, sports grounds and institutional land. Interestingly there are none in the inner city between the Royal and Grand Canals, east of the Phoenix Park, and there may in fact never have been hedgerows in this area.

Hedges are a particularly important wildlife habitat and are a reservoir for native Irish plant species in the city area. A biodiversity survey carried out in November 2006 revealed the presence of 144 species of plants, 99 of which were native Irish species. Dublin City's hedges contain Crab apple, holly, oak, hazel, primrose, Dog violets, Lords and ladies, Wild rose, woodbine and colourful Herb Robert as well as Robin-run-the-hedge – the sticky plant so beloved of schoolchildren. Nettles and ivy are in every hedge while such hedge specials as Wild garlic and Lesser celandine can be found with a bit of hunting.

Aerial shot of St Anne's park
inset: detail

Aerial shot of Phoenix Park

There are remnants of old woodland in some of our larger city parks, such as the Phoenix Park, St Anne's Park, Bushy Park, Marlay Park and St Enda's and this is where more typical woodland plants, such as Wood sorrel, Arum lily, bluebell and Wood anemone can be found. These woodland areas are home to species of fern, such as Hart's tongue and the Male fern, while in the more moist parts the tree trunks as well as the woodland floor will have a cover of mosses.

FUNGI

In autumn time in particular, woodland areas are full of the smells and fruiting bodies of our fungi – mushrooms and toadstools. One of the most pungent is the stinkhorn *Phallus impudicus* which can give off a smell like a blocked sewer – apparently to attract flies that spread its spores. Clumps of small mushrooms are frequently seen. They grow on decomposing timber and on decaying leaves and are very important in helping to break down and recycle dead plant material. Lawns and grassy areas often have rings of mushrooms growing there. These live on dead grass roots and spread out in circles with each passing year. Indeed some of Dublin's mushroom species are edible while others are deadly poisonous. Unless one is absolutely sure of their identification it is best to avoid eating any of them.

Puffball – a meal for a slug!

Phallus impudicus

Waxcap

Gills of Pleurotus species

The variety of wildlife in Dublin's parks and gardens is a reflection of the variety of uses to which they are put. Parks and gardens can have planted areas of shrubs and flowerbeds. Introduced species here – whether it be welcome species, such as heavily berried *Pyracantha* bushes or nasty creatures such as the pine weevil which arrived in the soil of potted plants bought from garden centres – will interact with the true Dubs, whose ancestors were here before the City itself, such as hazel and willow trees and blackbirds and thrushes. Throw into the mix the amount of construction and demolition that is a feature of urban areas, together with the changes becoming apparent because of the effects of global warming and one thing becomes clear: the wildlife of Dublin's parks and gardens will always be in a state of change. There will always be a few tales of the unexpected waiting to be noticed by the observant citizen.

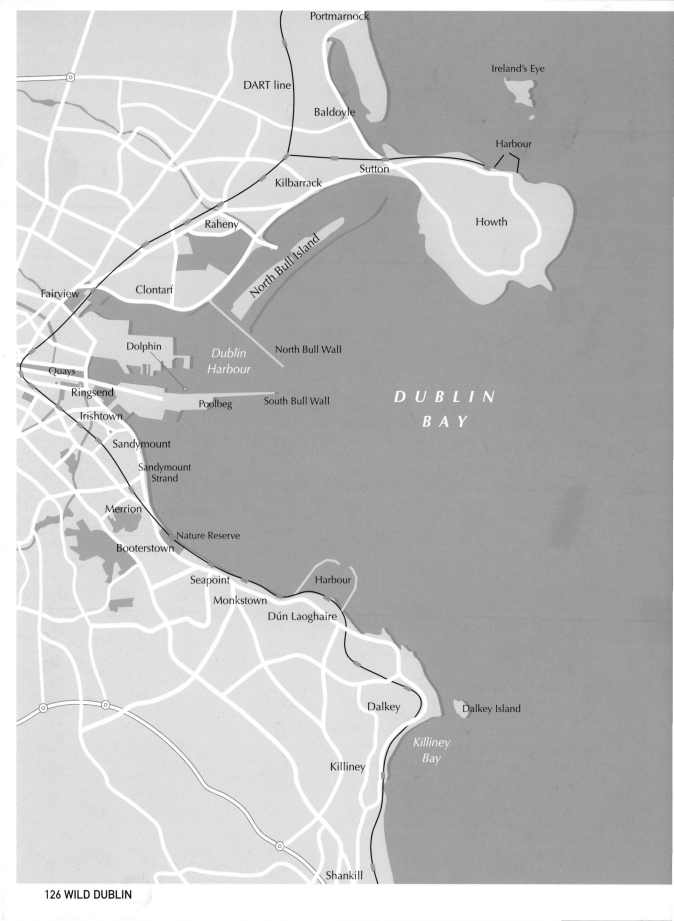

Portmarnock

Ireland's Eye

Baldoyle

Harbour

Sutton

Kilbarrack

Howth

Raheny

North Bull Island

Fairview

Clontarf

North Bull Wall

Dolphin

Dublin Harbour

Quays

Ringsend

Poolbeg

South Bull Wall

D U B L I N
B A Y

Irishtown

Sandymount

Sandymount Strand

Merrion

Nature Reserve

Booterstown

Seapoint

Harbour

Monkstown

Dún Laoghaire

Dalkey

Dalkey Island

Killiney Bay

Killiney

Shankill

CHAPTER FOUR

A TRIP ON THE DART TO SEE DUBLIN'S COASTLINE

Dublin's coastline contains a great variety of wildlife – from dolphins to snails, kestrels to wild goats – all can be spotted along the bay. Starting just north of Bray, the coastline sweeps north, around Sorrento Point into Dublin Bay, over the Liffey estuary and along by Bull Island to the isthmus at Sutton and thence on to the Howth promontory. A good way to explore this remarkable coastline is by DART – starting at Shankill and getting off at stations of interest along the way. Even if your trips on the DART are merely journeys to and from work, you cannot fail to be captivated by the abundance of wildlife that lives in our coastal zone and which varies with location and season.

The Dublin County boundary is the Dargle River, just north of Bray, and there is a green belt between that and Shankill, separating the built-up city of Dublin from the Wicklow hinterland. It is logical, therefore, that the trip along the city coastline should start at the DART Station in Shankill.

Once out of Shankill station, the sea quickly comes into view and this is the best section of the coastline – from here to Dalkey – to keep an eye out for sea mammals. While you won't exactly see these sea creatures from your train seat, they do occur occasionally off the coast where the DART is travelling. Seals, porpoises, dolphins or indeed whales can appear in these waters depending on the time of year.

SEA MAMMALS

CETACEANS – WHALES AND DOLPHINS

Cetaceans are mammals that are supremely adapted to life in the sea. They spend their entire lives there, breed, give birth and suckle their young without ever needing to come ashore. In fact, because the ocean supports their body weight, they can grow to enormous sizes. The largest animal that has ever existed on earth is the blue whale. The largest ever recorded was a female from the Antarctic that measured 33.5 metres long and weighed between 190 and 200 tonnes.

There are two sorts of cetaceans, distinguished by how they feed. Baleen whales feed by filtering great mouthfuls of seawater through baleen plates in their mouths. There are eleven species of baleen whale ranging from the largest – the Blue whale – right down to the smallest one – the Minke whale – which are often seen in Irish waters. There are sixty-eight species of toothed cetaceans including Sperm whales, Beaked whales, dolphins and porpoises. These use their teeth to catch individual items of prey.

Cetaceans communicate by sound. They use sonar to navigate and to detect prey. They can dive to considerable depths and remain submerged for a long time. But then they come to the surface, expel their breath though their blowhole – one or two depending on species – and take in a new breath before slipping beneath the waves again.

WHALES

Minke whale

Unlikely as it may seem, whales have been recorded in the Irish Sea very close to the Dublin coastline. The species seen is the Minke. This is the smallest whale that comes into Irish waters and the only species that ventures up the Irish Sea from time to time, in summer and autumn. The Minke whale is a Baleen whale, which means that it has baleen plates for filtering food from water rather than having teeth. It feeds at the surface and dines upon small fish as well as the smaller plankton. Its dives can last for twenty minutes or so and then it surfaces and blows the air from its lungs through its two blowholes on the top of its head.

It is the whale's blow that attracts the watcher's attention – two spouts rising to about 2 metres – not particularly spectacular. When it dives it just submerges itself – there are no acrobatics with its tail raised in the air, as happens with other species of whale. But it is very much a whale – much bigger than any other sea mammal you are likely to see off the Dublin coast – it can be up to 10 metres in length, which is far bigger than the next biggest sea mammal recorded in the Irish Sea – the Bottle-nosed dolphin.

...ıs

...in that have been spotted along ...lin Bay itself, just off the ...lphin and the big- ...sed can ...he ...ape of ...k with a well- ...e up to 4 metres long ...kilograms. Females are smaller – ... 3.2 metres in length but are distinctly more svelte at only 190 kilograms.

The Common dolphin is smaller, only up to 2.5 metres long, and is recognisable by the white markings on its sides, which have an hourglass shape – no doubt to emphasise its waistline!

Both dolphins are social animals and may appear in groups. They feed on fish at depth or at the surface. Both species have one blowhole on the top of their head and will blow when they surface from a dive, which might last up to ten minutes. While they can appear at any time of the year, the best months for sightings are between July and October.

Bottle-nosed dolphin

PORPOISES

The most common cetacean seen off the Dublin coast is the Harbour porpoise, also called the Common porpoise. This is a much smaller and fatter species than the dolphin as its Irish name *Muc mhara* – the sea pig – will attest. Females are bigger than the males in this species and can reach a length of 1.7 metres.

These are the easiest cetaceans to see and a walk along the coast will often yield sightings of two or three swimming along in an undulating fashion with their dark bodies and short triangular fin breaking the water as they loop along. They hardly ever jump clear of the water and prefer to rest by floating on the surface.

Sightings are most likely from June, throughout the autumn and winter. The skull of a specimen stranded on Sandymount Strand is on display in the Natural History Museum (on Merrion Street).

Bottle-nosed dolphins can sometimes attack porpoises – most dead specimens washed ashore show evidence of such attacks. The dolphins are not attacking them to kill them and eat them, so it is thought that they are fighting with them over food supplies, taking out sexual frustration on them or even just overdoing horseplay. You can form your own opinion, as these attacks are sometimes seen by observers on land!

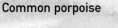
Common porpoise

Common seal

Common seals, Bull Island

SEALS

Seals differ from cetaceans in that while they are air-breathing mammals that feed and sleep at sea, they must come ashore to breed.

There are two species of seal in Irish waters, the Common seal and the Grey seal – which is in fact the more common of the two! The Grey seal is frequently seen all along the Dublin coastline. In fact the remains of one found in a Mesolithic midden on Dalkey Island were 6,400 years old. Obviously our hunter-gatherer forebears weren't confined to gathering shellfish.

The Grey seals are quite big and have a large flat head like a horse and what is described as a roman nose. They occur all along the east coast and are frequently seen. They are curious creatures and will bob up quite regularly to see what is going on. They may seem like nice friendly creatures – but swimmers should keep well clear of them as they are not above taking a curious bite out of a swimmer that ventures too near.

A close encounter with a large bull Grey seal, which can weigh up to 300 kilograms is not amusing. They eat up to 10 kilograms of food per day, which includes fish, crustaceans, squid and any seabirds they can nab from underneath the water surface.

Grey seals breed on Dalkey Island and on Lambay Island. Pupping, which is the word for breeding, happens between September and November.

Common seals are smaller than Grey seals and have an upturned nose more like that of a dog in profile. They can occasionally turn up in the area too as they have a breeding colony on Bull Island as we shall see when we make it round the coast to there.

Anyway, enough of this craning your neck to see spots and specks on the sea – we are now approaching Killiney station and it's time to get out.

KILLINEY BEACH

Killiney Beach has been compared to the Bay of Naples – with the sweep of the bay backed by the Dublin and Wicklow mountains. This opinion certainly holds true for the vista from the mail boat at sea, but it is still nonetheless a magnificent scene as you gaze at it from the railway bridge at Killiney station. Down on the beach you will quickly become aware that this is a grey, stony, pebbly beach rather than an expanse of golden sand. The shore shelves steeply, giving depth almost immediately to swimmers and it is well worth going for a swim as this is one of Dublin's Blue Flag beaches.

Killiney Beach

BLUE FLAG BEACHES

The Blue Flag programme is an international scheme, devised to award flags of excellence to beaches which achieve the highest quality standards. In 2007, eighty Irish beaches and three marinas received the award. In Dublin County the Blue Flag beaches were: Portrane, Donabate, Killiney and Seapoint. To achieve a Blue Flag, beaches have to meet twenty-nine criteria in the following areas: environmental, education and information, water quality, environmental management, safety and services.

Dollymount beach received its Blue Flag for the first time in 2005. This was the first time that a bathing area in the Dublin City area was awarded a Blue Flag, and Ireland is one of only five countries that has had a Blue Flag beach within its capital city. There had been a significant improvement in the water quality in Dublin Bay since 2003, due mainly to the new Wastewater Treatment Plant at Ringsend. However, a small number of samples from Dollymount in 2006 and again in 2007 did not meet the very high standards set for Blue Flags. Bathing water at Dollymount does, however, meet all the standards specified for safe bathing water by the Local Authorities.

Seapoint

A walk along the shoreline will reveal interesting items washed up by the tide. Every summer jellyfish swim up the Irish Sea and several of these can be washed ashore. In fact, in 2005 such an amount of Lion's mane jellyfish came in that the beaches were closed for a period. Jellyfish are very primitive animals – they have no blood system or excretory system. They have a saucer-shaped jelly-like body and several mouths that hang as arms under the body as it floats in the sea. These mouth arms are surrounded by stinging tentacles, which paralyse any small creature that may be in the vicinity. They are then swept into the mouths as food. They may also have tentacles hanging in a circle all around the perimeter of the jellyfish body as extra stinging cells. No wonder an encounter with one in the sea can be unpleasant for a swimmer. Here (seen below) washed up on the shore is the Common jellyfish. This has a transparent body up to 25 centimetres in diameter with four blue circles. Even though it is now dead, the tentacles can retain their stinging ability for a considerable time. The Lion's mane jellyfish is a much larger animal, which can be up to 50 centimetres across, with large mouth arms and many vicious stinging tentacles hanging from its undersides. The problem with jellyfish in the water is that if the tentacles are cut off, say by the propeller of a boat, they will still give a swimmer a nasty sting across the face while the swimmer will not see them to avoid them.

Common jellyfish, Bull Island

Along the shore you might encounter the wonderfully-named mermaid's purse. This is a brown rectangular-shaped empty object that looks like a hardened piece of brown seaweed, which has a long twisted string on each corner. It can be up to 8 centimetres long and is, in fact, the egg case of the dogfish. The eggs were inside this in the sea and the whole contraption was tied by the tendrils to seaweed. The eggs have long since hatched and departed and the egg case was broken free by tide and storm and deposited here on the beach. But keep your eyes peeled for mermaids just in case!

FLOTSAM AND JETSAM

Flotsam is, by definition, wreckage found floating, whereas jetsam is cargo jettisoned overboard to lighten a ship's load in times of difficulty. In modern usage, flotsam also includes driftwood and other natural debris in the sea.

Another bit of flotsam you may encounter is a collection of whelk egg cases. This is like a piece of yellow bubble-wrap, and indeed it is hard to believe that it was once part of a living thing. It was, however, the maternity unit for the Common whelk, a single-shelled snail-like creature that lives in deeper waters. Again the eggs have already hatched out by the time this mass of egg cases has been washed up on the shore.

You can even try your hand at long-line fishing from the shore at the permitted times. Such fish species as bass, coalfish, codling and plaice are lounging about on the bottom just waiting to be tempted by a tasty bait. These fish frequent shallow coastal waters and can be caught if you are patient. On the other hand, you could return to the station and hop on the next DART, which will take you through the tunnel and on to Dalkey station.

Whelk egg cases. Killiney

DALKEY

There are two interesting wildlife areas within reach from Dalkey station – Dalkey Quarry and Dalkey Island. Dalkey gets its name from the Blackthorn Tree. The original name of Dalkey Island was *Delg-inis* – thorn island. The Danes had a fortress here in the tenth century and they changed the word *Delg* into their word for thorn, which was *Dalk,* and changed the word *inis* to the northern word for an island – *ey*.

Dalkey Quarry is a granite quarry. The stone from here was quarried to build Dún Laoghaire Harbour and the Great South Wall.

The quarry has long been abandoned to wildlife and to intrepid rock climbers, who practise their skills on the high back walls. The floor of the quarry has become overgrown with dense thickets of briars and gorse, with sycamore and ash trees forming a canopy. Kestrels nest on the cliff as well as a pair of Peregrine falcons, who reared two chicks here in 2006. The ground flora supports colonies of bumble bees and butterflies, such as the meadow brown and the ringlet.

Dalkey Island is more difficult to reach. Swimming across is not at all advisable as there

Peregrine falcon flying over Dún
Laoghaire Harbour

is a strong tidal current that rips over and back, as the tides flow into and out of Dublin Bay. Better try your luck at Coliemore Harbour and see if you can go out by boat. As you sail over from Coliemore to Dalkey Island, you cross the sea bed which shelves deeply in the centre and then rises up again to form Dalkey Island. Behind Dalkey Island are the rocks known as the Muglins, and the best area for scuba diving in the whole bay is around this area.

   Traditionally the water of Dublin Bay has been rich in organic material. This was food for the filter-feeding animals, which thrived in the midst of such plenty. The whole bottom of the sea all across to Dalkey Island is carpeted with mussels – easily recognisable by their purple-black bivalve shells. These filter the water of Dublin Bay and absorb the organic content of the water. Before the upgrading of the Ringsend Wastewater Treatment Plant, much of the organic matter in Dublin Bay originated from sewage. The mussels didn't mind – they filtered it into their bodies together with any associated bacteria that might accompany it. The short time needed to cook mussels is not long enough to kill bacteria – so it was no wonder that poor Molly Malone died of a fever. It may well have been typhoid fever, which is carried by bacteria that were probably excreted into Dublin Bay by a previous carrier in Molly Malone's time in the eighteenth century.

In fact, eating filter-feeding shellfish from any kind of questionable waters is never to be recommended. In James Joyce's *Ulysses*, Leopold Bloom muses on the sad fate of an O'Connor family, who died after being poisoned by mussels from Dublin Bay. This is, in fact, a true incident. In June 1890 the O'Connor children were sent to gather mussels, and instead of going to the seashore, as they were told, they collected them from a contaminated pool at Seapoint. Their mother, their servant and three of the children died that evening from eating the mus-sels that obviously contained nasty bacteria derived from sewage.

Anyway, the trip to Dalkey Island is to see the wild goats. This is the only place in the whole county of Dublin where wild goats can be seen. These goats were originally brought here by humans, but are now completely feral and breed and look after themselves without any interference. Their browsing habit of feeding keeps the island from being overgrown with scrub. Goats spend their days alternating between feeding in the open and resting in shelter, so they are not all that difficult to spot.

The next stop of wildlife interest is Dún Laoghaire, so back to the DART for three more stations and get off at Dún Laoghaire Pier.

Feral goats on Dalkey Island
Left: Kestrel, Dalkey

Pomarine skua in Dún Laoghaire, summer 2006

DÚN LAOGHAIRE

Dún Laoghaire Harbour was built between 1814 and 1848 – and was the largest artificial harbour in the world at the time. The East Pier is 1 kilometre long, while the West Pier is 1.5 kilometres, and they enclose a harbour of 102 hectares. The harbour was built with blocks of granite hewn from Dalkey Quarry and transported on a gravity-fed tramway, which ran along the same route as the DART follows today. A great range of seabirds, or indeed human wildlife, can be observed from either pier.

Many of our common seabirds can be easily seen, in particular Sea-ducks and waders. In winter, look out for turnstones, turning over the Bladder wrack. The celebrity bird is the Purple sandpiper, another winter visitor, so well camouflaged against the dark stone and seaweed that you really have to look closely to see it.

Gulls are there in abundance, feeding in the harbour and at sea. Their breeding colonies, however, are further afield on Bray Head, Lambay Island, Howth and Ireland's Eye, although some herring gulls have taken to nesting on chimney pots in the centre of Dublin. Our largest gull – the Greater black-backed gull – can be seen from the piers all year round. The Lesser black-backed gull is a summer migrant, and is mainly seen between March and the end of October. However, some can be seen during winter months too as they don't all go. You will, of course, spot the difference between the two with careful observation. Lesser black-backs are smaller, their backs (the folded wings) are slate grey and their legs are yellow. Greater black-backed gulls are larger, their backs are jet black and their legs are pink.

Greater black-backed gull
Inset: Lesser black-backed gulls

Next in size is the Herring gull – quite a substantial bird at 56-66 centimetres. This is the typical seagull that everyone is familiar with. It has a light grey back, black wing tips and white feathers everywhere else. It has pink legs and a yellow bill. Like the Black-backed gulls it too has a red dot on its bill during the breeding season. The young know to peck at this spot to stimulate the parent into regurgitating food from its crop for their meal. Black-headed gulls are easily identified. In the breeding season they have a splendid black head, which is part of their breeding plumage. At least, it looks black, although in fact the feathers are dark brown. In winter, however, they lose these dark feathers and all that remains is a dark ear spot – but they are still easy to pick out.

The kittiwake is about the same size as the Black-headed gull – about 40 centimetres. This is a slender gull with a completely white head, grey back, black wing tips and dark-grey legs. It got its name from its call: 'Kit-i-wak, Kit-i-wak', but it won't always be calling when you see it at Dún Laoghaire – its call is usually heard at the breeding cliffs of Howth and Bray Head. If you walk right down to the lighthouse at the end of the pier, you may come across fulmars. These birds are not actually gulls but look like them with their grey backs and yellowish bills. They do not have black wing tips and they have black patches on their heads in front of their eyes. They fly on stiff wings with a long gliding flight and stiff-wing beats.

Several other species of gulls turn up from time to time, to the delight of the twitchers (bird watchers) – Iceland gull, Mediterranean gull, Common gull, to mention but a few. However, any observant walker should see the five usual species described here without any difficulty.

From top clockwise: Kittiwake, Black-headed gull, Great black-backed gull, Lesser black-backed gull and Herring gull

In summer you will see other white screeching seabirds that are too elegant and fast flying for gulls. These are terns – seabirds that are so totally adapted to life at sea that they can feed, sleep and mate there with no need to come ashore. However, laying eggs at sea is a non-runner, so these birds visit the coast of Dublin during the summer months. There are five species of tern that breed in Ireland, and four of them breed along the Dublin coast – the Common tern, the Arctic tern, the Little tern and the Roseate tern, which breeds on Rockabill. The Sandwich tern breeds in Strangford Lough, further north, but it flies south along the coast in summer too. In Dún Laoghaire the terns you are most likely to see in summer are the Sandwich tern, the Common and the Arctic tern. The latter two are almost impossible to tell apart in flight but you certainly wouldn't mix them up with seagulls. They have red legs, a red-pointed bill, a black head and the rest of their feathers are brilliant white. They have long slender wings and a forked tail, giving them the nickname sea swallows. The Sandwich tern is much noisier and will probably come to your attention first. It too has a black head, but differs from the others in having black legs and a black bill.

From top clockwise: Sandwich tern, Roseate tern, Arctic tern, Common tern and Little tern

Occasionally there comes a report that a penguin has been seen off Dún Laoghaire pier. This is never the case: what is being reported is a guillemot or a razorbill, both of which turn up here from time to time. These birds spend all their time in the water around the piers and have the typical black plumage above and white plumage below of the auk family to which they belong. They can be differentiated from each other by their beaks: the guillemot has a pointed bill, whereas that of the razorbill is so called because it resembles a cut-throat razor. Penguins cannot fly at all and only live in the southern hemisphere. The only way you could see one in Dún Laoghaire is if one was smuggled here from Dublin Zoo.

While you are looking over the wall out to sea, you may observe black long-necked birds swimming on the water that suddenly disappear in a dive and stay under for up to a minute. These are either cormorants or shags. Cormorants are the bigger of the two, and if you get a good look at them, you will see that they have a white patch on their face and another on their thigh, as it were. The shag is smaller, all black, and in the breeding season has what can only be described as a Mohican hairstyle on the top of its head – a crest of upright feathers. These birds often take to the wing and fly in a characteristic flight with outstretched neck. Perched on land or on a rocky outcrop they stand

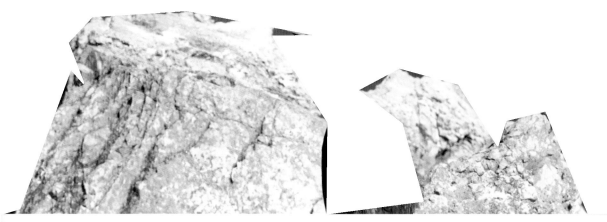

with wings outstretched, as if they were trying to dry their wings, though apparently such a pose is merely to help them digest their latest meal of fish.

Another bird you are likely to see in summer is the gannet, as there is a gannet colony on Ireland's Eye. This is our largest breeding sea bird. It has a gleaming white body, black wing tips, a yellow head and very efficient blue eyes. In fact its Latin name *Sula* derives from the Irish word for eye – súil – in recognition of its excellent ability to see fish in the water from a great height and therefore to dive on the shoal with its 2-metre wings folded back to form a living arrowhead.

Skuas are the pirates of the seabird world. They harry other seabirds until they disgorge their last meal, which is still in their crop, and feed on the food as it drops from the molested victim. Skuas are occasionally spotted off the Dublin coast as spring and autumn passage migrants – they breed in Northern Europe in summer and spend the winter in the south Atlantic. A Pomarine skua was seen hunting along the Dublin coast in July 2007, while Arctic skuas and Great skuas have been recorded off the Dublin coast in autumn and spring.

On your way back up the pier you may encounter some Rock pipits: small, streaky lark-like birds, which hop among the breakwater stones on the seaward side. These feed on sand-hoppers, snails and slugs and nest in crevasses in the rocks. You could also encounter such opportunists as Grey crows and starlings, as these forage for food in any type of habitat where free food might be available. Indeed, you could even startle a Brown rat or two foraging among the breakwater stones looking for food.

But now it's back to the DART and on to the rocky shore at Seapoint. Once you leave Dún Laoghaire, the DART is now skirting Dublin Bay proper. Dublin Bay is internationally important for wildlife and has been designated as such under the European Birds Directive and Habitats Directive. The bay is such a wealth of biodiversity within the confines of our capital city and is accessible to all by the DART.

EU DIRECTIVES

Two EU Directives have been responsible for the designation of areas for the protection and conservation of wildlife.

The Birds Directive of 1979 requires that areas, designated as Special Protection Areas (SPAs), be set aside for the protection of birds that are important on a European scale and listed as such in its Annexe 1. It also requires that wetlands which attract one per cent or more of the international population of that species, or more than 20,000 birds, be designated as SPAs. As of 2006, Ireland has 127 designated SPAs. There are three in the area covered by this book: Sandymount Strand/Tolka Estuary, North Bull Island and Howth Head Coast.

The Habitats Directive of 1992 requires that sites be designated as Special Areas of Conservation (SACs) for the conservation of natural and semi-natural habitats and species of flora and fauna that are important on a European scale. This directive lists habitats and species which must be protected. As of 2006, Ireland has identified 413 candidate SACs and notified the European Commission. Following agreement with the Commission, they will be formally declared Special Areas of Conservation. There are three in the area covered by this book: North Dublin Bay, South Dublin Bay and Howth Head.

Opposite left: Cormorants, Seapoint
Above: Young comorants
Inset: Brown rat, Seapoint

SEAPOINT

A nice rocky stretch of coastline lies just north of the Martello tower at Seapoint. You can get right down to it through steps in the wall and if you pick the right time, when the tide is low, a good expanse of rocky shore and rock pools are there for your exploration.

Rocky shore, Seapoint

ABOUT THE TIDES

The tide goes in and out twice every day because of the gravitational force on the earth caused by the sun and the moon. There are two things to consider about the tides when visiting a rocky shore. First is whether the tide is in or out. Tides take approximately six hours and thirteen minutes to come in, and the same time to go out. High tide today will be just fifty-two minutes later than it was yesterday. For example, the tide could be fully in at 09.40 yesterday and again at 22.06, whereas today it will be full tide at 10.32 and again at 22.58.

Secondly, the height of the tide varies throughout the month depending on the help the moon gives the sun with exerting gravitational force. When the sun and the moon are in a straight line relative to the earth – as happens at new moon and full moon – the force is greatest. The tides at these times are called spring tides and the range is greatest. The full tide could be up to five metres high (above ordnance datum) and will cover the whole foreshore. When these tides go out they will drop right back to 0.2 metres and expose the whole lower shore – hence this is a very good time to see all the wildlife on the rocky shore.

When the sun and moon are at right angles to each other relative to the earth, as happens at the first and third quarters of the moon, there is less gravitational force. The tides at this time are called neap tides, and the range is much lower. The tide won't come in as far, or go out as far: high tide could be 3 metres and low tide 1.5 metres. There is much less shore exposed at this time of the month. Stormy weather can also affect the height of the high tide, for example, if there is a strong on-shore wind behind it, blowing it up on to the coast.

LIFE ON A ROCKY SHORE

There are essentially two problems with living on a rocky shore: being moved and being exposed. To combat movement, much of the life on the shore is stuck fast on the rocks so that they cannot be torn off. The rest have round shapes so that they can roll around quite safely during wave action without being damaged. The second problem is exposure while the tide is out. This means that there is a danger of drying out, and worse still for an animal, a risk of starvation. Food arrives with the tidal water and these animals can only feed when they are covered in water. So, naturally, there is much more seashore life on the lower shore and in rocky pools than on the rocks on the upper shore.

SEAWEEDS

Seaweeds – or algae – come in three colours: green, brown and red. Green algae grow on the upper shore where they have the most light. Here you will most commonly encounter Sea lettuce *Ulva lactuca*, which has a flat, very thin green frond and Link frond *Enteromorpha spp.* They are not confined here, of course, but as they can tolerate fresh water in the form of rain, they tend to occupy the upper shore, which is left exposed for long periods.

A good range of brown seaweeds occur on the middle shore. When the tide is out these look like floppy bundles stuck to the rocks. However, when the tide is in they are able to rise up vertically because they have air bladders in their fronds, and they wave about under water like a mini forest. There is a pecking order here too and some are able to hack the vicissitudes of the higher shore better than others. The order they occur in tends to be as follows:

Bladder wrack, Seapoint

Channel wrack *Pelvetia canaliculata*
– rolled-in fronds which look like channels.
Spiral wrack *Fucus spiralis*
– hold it up and it will hang in a spiral.
Knotted wrack *Ascophyllum nodosum*
– very thin with large air bladders.
Bladder wrack *Fucus vesiculosus*
– much broader than the last, with air bladders.
Serrated wrack *Fucus serratus*
– edges of fronds definitely serrated,
with no bladders.
Kelp *Laminaria spp.*
– large thick straps with holdfasts at the end.

Knotted wrack

Carrageen moss

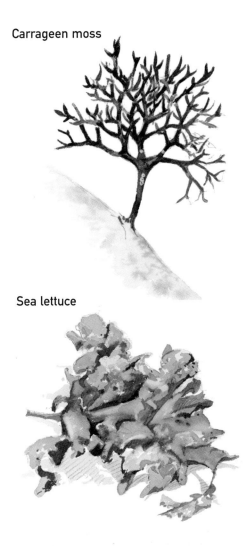

Sea lettuce

The red seaweeds are a more delicate group. They grow in deeper water and are usually found washed up on the shore, broken in bits by the waves. They can include such things as Laver *Porphyra spp.*, which looks like red sea lettuce, Dulse *Palmaria palmata* and Carrageen moss *Chondrus crispus*. Dried dulse is a very popular snack in the West of Ireland – it is sold in small packets and nibbled appreciatively by the cognoscenti. Laver is highly prized in Wales and Laverbread is a local breakfast speciality. A substitute for gelatine is abstracted from Carrageen moss when it is boiled with milk and the resultant milk jelly formed a very important part of the diet of coastal populations fadó. Seaweed is also popular in seaweed baths offered to visitors in Clare and Sligo; the brown wracks are used in seaweed baths for their mucilaginous qualities. You may also find bits of calcareous pink algae growing on rocks on the lower shore. The red pigment helps them to grow at the lower light intensities experienced under water.

Where you get plants you get animals, and the rocky shore is a very interesting place to look for these. Like the plants, they too have their special places to live, depending on how well they can tolerate the arduous rocky shore conditions. The first animals you will probably encounter are the barnacles – those white encrustations that feel so sharp if you have the misfortune to clamber over a rock covered with them in your bare feet. They are permanently cemented on to the rock and no tide or storm will dislodge them. They have an opening in their roof, which they keep firmly closed when the tide is out. When they are covered with seawater they open the roof, put out their legs and kick any nearby floating food into their mouths.

Winkles, Seapoint

You are much further down the shore when you encounter the limpets. These are also stuck to the rocks to prevent desiccation when the tide is gone. They, however, leave their spot when covered with water and go around grazing the green algae off the rocks – the cows of the shore, as it were.

If you look under the brown seaweeds you will find several different species of periwinkles. The edible periwinkle *Littorina littorea*, familiar to those who dine on such delicacies – gathered from a much cleaner source than Dublin Bay – lives on the middle shore. It can close the little door on the bottom of its shell – the *operculum* – when the tide is out and open it again to feed when covered with water. The periwinkles on the upper shore are much smaller, as they have less time to feed. The species you may find here are the Black periwinkle *Littorina neritoide* and the Rough periwinkle *L. saxatilis*. Down lower on the shore you will find the flat periwinkle *L. obtusata*, sometimes called *L. littoralis*, a small, flat, usually yellow winkle.

There are other snail-like creatures here too. Those that live in beautifully coloured stripy shells are called top shells, and the purple one *Gibbula umbilicalis* is the one most often seen. Others of these snail-like animals are carnivores and prey on their more sedentary neighbours. Dog whelks *Nucella lapillus* fall into this category. They bore holes into unsuspecting barnacles and limpets using acid, which they produce, and then suck out the contents. They have a definite groove on the underside of the shell and are much more robust than periwinkles.

Starfish, Seapoint

There are bivalves on the shore here – animals with two shells, which they keep too tightly closed when the tide is out. The most common one is the mussel *Mytilus edulis*, which holds on to the rocks with its byssus threads. Other bivalve shells you may find here, such as cockles and razor shells, have been washed in empty by the tide. These creatures live on different shores in Dublin Bay. You may find the sworn deadly enemy of the mussel here too – the starfish – or at least a dead one that may have been washed up from deeper waters further out in the bay, where the sea bottom is carpeted both with mussels and starfish feeding on them. On the underside of their arms starfish have rows of small tube feet with suckers. By grabbing on to the mussels with these, a starfish can pull them open. It then extrudes its stomach out of its mouth, which is in the centre of its body, and inserts it into the hapless mussel. Then, with its digestive juices, it absorbs the mussel meat. This gory operation happens in the sea so you are hardly likely to witness it here on the rocky shore at Seapoint.

Look in any rock pools you may encounter and examine the sides of them for anemones

Hermit crab, Seapoint

Actinia spp. stuck to the rocks. These are animals, although they may look like flowers when covered in water. They use their tentacles to filter in water and trap and eat any creatures thus sucked up. Try putting your finger in one to feel the pull. If they get uncovered by water, they can contract their tentacles to look like a blob of half-sucked fruit pastille. You will also find shore crabs in the rock pools, as they really must be in water all the time, or at least sheltering under very wet seaweed. The common shore crab *Carcinus maenas* can be green, yellow, brown or even black in colour as it is a master of camouflage. It is both a carnivore and a scavenger of dead things and will give you a right nip if you lift it up the wrong way.

Of the birds that you so carefully identified on Dún Laoghaire Harbour – many, such as gulls, will feed here or rest on nearby rocks. Keep an eye open for them, but while you are trespassing on their habitat they will keep a safe distance.

It's time to get the next DART to Booterstown.

Aerial shot of Booterstown Marsh

BOOTERSTOWN

Booterstown Marsh, 4 hectares in area, was really created when the first Irish railway line – the Dublin to Kingstown line – was built in 1834. The line was laid on a stone-faced embankment from Merrion to Blackrock at the edge of the coastal saltmarsh. Most of the area between that and the Merrion Road has been filled up since then, for instance, Blackrock Park, which is well above sea level. However, Booterstown Marsh remains at the height of the high tides. It is a brackish marsh – not a full saltmarsh – as the Trimleston Stream coming down from Mount Merrion and the Elm Park Stream both enter the sea here and the fresh and salt waters mix in Booterstown Marsh. It originally had tidal flaps in the embankment that opened outwards to let the freshwater out, but closed against the incoming tide to keep the salt water out. However, the flaps get jammed open with beach deposits and salt water has been able to flow into the marsh, increasing the salinity of the water and indeed spreading any pollution in the inflowing streams across the marsh.

The marsh is now in the Dún Laoghaire-Rathdown Council area, and over the years maintenance works have been undertaken by them or their predecessors. It has freshwater-marsh plants, such as watercress, Great willow herb and Water horsetail. It also has true salt-marsh plants, such as Glasswort and Sea purslane. It also has stands of vegetation that grows in brackish conditions – stands of Sea Club-rush, Grey Club-rush and Saltmarsh rush. In particular, it contains a species of saltmarsh grass that is exceedingly rare in Ireland and which is listed as a protected species under our 2000 Wildlife Act – Borrer's Saltmarsh Grass.

The marsh is important for wading birds, many of which roost here when high tides cover the mud flats on Dublin Bay. Common snipe, in particular, use it to over-winter. The marsh is also a popular spot for herons. An oil spill in the

Redshank and curlew, Seapoint

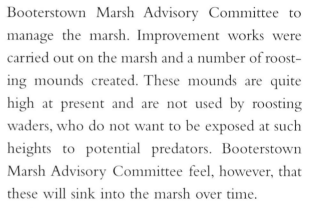

1980s had reduced the value of the marsh for long billed waders, but recent counts by the Irish Wetland Bird Survey showed that by 2000 the marsh had recovered. Black-tailed Godwits and Curlew were being recorded there again, as well as Redshank and Dunlin, and ducks such as teal. In fact, the number of wading birds using it has doubled each year since 2000. Some snipe have been recorded here too during the winter of 2006.

The Williamstown Stream flows parallel to the sea wall just south of the marsh and kingfishers fly along this with a thrilling flash of turquoise iridescence. It is well worth looking out for these birds as they fly parallel to the railway line and can be seen from the DART.

An Taisce now own the lease and manage the marsh. In 2006 the local An Taisce group and Friends of Booterstown (a local residents' group) came together under the umbrella title of Booterstown Marsh Advisory Committee to manage the marsh. Improvement works were carried out on the marsh and a number of roosting mounds created. These mounds are quite high at present and are not used by roosting waders, who do not want to be exposed at such heights to potential predators. Booterstown Marsh Advisory Committee feel, however, that these will sink into the marsh over time.

The Irish Wetland Birds counts for 2006 show that the wader and waterfowl numbers using the marsh appear not to have been detrimentally affected by the works, though it may of course take several years for the full picture to emerge. Keep an eye out as you go through Booterstown station. Niall Hatch at Birdwatch Ireland, who collates all the bird data for the Irish Wetlands Survey, will welcome your observations. But now it's back on the DART and off to Sandymount.

SANDYMOUNT STRAND

When you make your way from the DART to Sandymount Strand, bear in mind that you are approaching one of the most acclaimed strands in literature. At the beginning of the twentieth century when Stephen Dedalus, the hero of *Ulysses*, was taking his walk along the strand and wondering, 'Am I walking into eternity along Sandymount Strand?' the strand in fact stretched all the way to Ringsend. Construction, landfill and reclamation on the South Bull mud flats have reduced the size of Sandymount Strand. However, they have created Ringsend Park, Sean Moore Park, Irishtown Nature Park and indeed the South Wall in the early eighteenth century, as well as the South Docklands area.

This is a muddy strand, exposed when the tide is out, so the animals that live here have to have a lifestyle that prevents them drying out and dying. What they do is burrow in the muddy sand and lie low until the tide, bearing food and protection, returns. Three very common species of marine worms – the lugworm, the ragworm and the sand mason – lurk beneath the muddy sand.

The lugworm *Arenicola marina* betrays its presence with a coiled conspicuous worm cast on the surface above where it is. This is a large worm, which can be up to 20 centimetres long and is as thick as a pencil. Like the earthworm on land, it swallows great quantities of the material it burrows into and digests any edible material that is in it, before excreting the unwanted bulk. As there is plenty of organic matter in the mud on Sandymount, there are lots and lots of lugworms. If you look closely at the worm cast and the place where it is, you will see a shallow depression in the sand near to the cast. This is where the head end of the worm is. A U-shaped

Sandymount Strand

tunnel connects this to the cast and the lugworm occupies this tunnel. But you will have to have a big shovel and move very fast if you want to dig one up for inspection, or to use as fishing bait, for this worm can burrow like lightning if it feels under attack. As it never leaves its burrow how does it meet other lugworms and reproduce? This creature is so well adapted to its harsh environment that it has an almost military strategy for reproduction. During the first fortnight in October each year, the lugworms come into season (as it were), and after a spell of rough weather at this time they liberate their eggs and sperm into the water above them. In such conditions fertilisation of the eggs is ensured and the next generation of Sandymount lugworms comes into being.

The carnivorous ragworms *Nereis diversicolor* are convoluted-looking worms that have sharp teeth and are not above biting the hand of anyone that catches them. This worm has a red line down its back and lives in and on top of the muddy sand. The fishermen digging for bait find it more difficult to catch than the lugworm, as it frequents more gravelly sand and rocky places. It eats other worms, small shrimps and anything else it can capture. Both species are beloved of wading birds and fishermen, so they keep themselves well hidden.

The sand mason *Lanice conchilega* is the third common worm species here. This is a tube worm that builds a sandy tube up to 30 centimetres long about its body. Protected by this it can poke itself up above the sand and filter feed from the open top of the tube when the tide is in. However, when the tide is out it feels

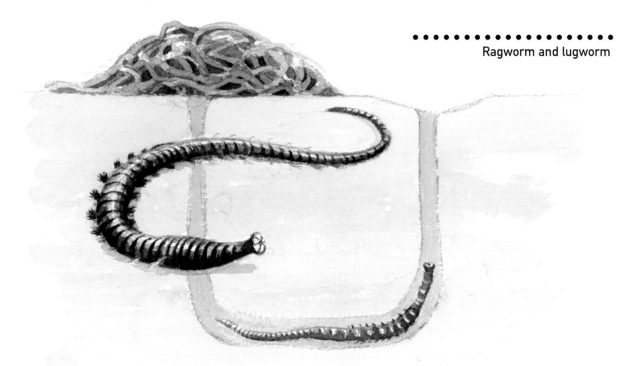

• • • • • • • • • • • • • • • • • • •
Ragworm and lugworm

Digging for lugworms, Sandymount
Right: Razor shells, Sandymount

exposed on the beach and withdraws itself far down its tube, leaving just the empty top 2.5 centimetres of sand tube sticking up above the sand. It can tunnel very fast so digging in the vicinity of the sandy tube is unlikely to produce a live specimen – unless of course you are a curlew with a long bill!

Another resident of Sandymount Strand is the cockle *Cerastoderma edule*. This is a bivalve – a two-shelled mollusc – and it lives buried in the muddy sand about 3 centimetres below the surface. When the tide comes in it opens the shells and puts up two siphons into the seawater above. It feeds and breathes through these. When the tide goes out it withdraws the siphons, closes the two shells tightly, battening down the hatches, as it were, and waits until the tide returns with its next feed. You'd

have to be a bird with a very strong beak indeed to remove and open a cockle, but the oystercatcher can do it.

Razor shells *Ensis ensis* also live in muddy sand. They are so called because the shells resembled the old cut-throat razors used for shaving long ago. These are also bivalve molluscs – the two shells enclosing a very strong muscle indeed, which make for tough eating. These also live buried in the sandy mud and wait for the tide to come in. They are filter-feeders and use their siphon to extract particles of food from the covering seawater. They live very near the surface, as their siphon is very short. However, if they feel any disturbance they can rapidly pull themselves deeper into the sand with their strong muscular foot, so catching them by digging for them is a skilled occupation. Crafty shellfish pickers know that if they pour salt down the hole left when the tide goes out, then they will be much easier to catch.

The Baltic tellin *Macoma balthica* is another mud-dwelling bivalve that occurs in the muddier parts of the sand. It too uses its siphon to draw down food from the surface when the tide is in. As the sea can bring along much by way of edible particles, great numbers of these can occur together where the feeding is good.

While cockles and razor shells are edible for humans too it is only advisable to eat them if they come from very clean pollution-free waters.

Sandymount is very important for Brent geese, specifically the light-bellied sub-species. These are visitors from the Canadian Arctic that first feed on the bed of Eelgrass that occurs at the eastern end (around the Merrion Gates) when they arrive in early October. They move on over the winter to feed on green algae, such as sea lettuce *Ulva lactuca* that occurs more widely and they roost on all the grassy places around the area when the tide is in. These geese occur here in winter in internationally important numbers – 3,361 birds were counted in January 2007 by the Irish Wetland Bird Survey.

The shore is much muddier on the north side of the Liffey Estuary at Bull Island, so this is the place to go to see the full range of wading birds that probe in soft mud. But before heading off there, take a brisk walk along Sandymount Strand, round the corner by Sean Moore Park and Irishtown Nature Park and out along the South Wall – if the sea is not rough and the waves are not high. It's a great two-hour walk.

Brent geese

Oystercatchers, Sandymount

SEAN MOORE PARK

This park came into being as a result of reclamation works and road building. It consists mainly of football pitches for the local football clubs. These are frequented by flocks of more than 300 Brent geese in winter, who feed on the grass. Flocks of up to 40 oystercatchers probe the soft wet pitches in winter for worms to supplement their diet. The north side of the park is bounded by a fine hedge of trees and shrubs and is frequented by songbirds in spring. The walk goes along the eastern boundary of the park and leads to Irishtown Nature Park.

IRISHTOWN NATURE PARK

This park must be one of Dublin's hidden treasures. Once an old domestic waste tiphead, it was developed in the 1980s as a Nature Park by the Parks Department, Dublin City Council and, apart from all the wildlife it now contains, it provides wonderful views all over Dublin Bay from its highest point. On a clear day there is a 360-degree view from the Dublin Mountains to Dalkey Island, to the South and North Walls, to Howth and across the north side of the city. Song birds such as linnet, greenfinch, goldfinch, Meadow pipit, stonechat and skylark can be spotted most of the year. Birds of prey, such as the kestrel, hunt mice and shrews and the raven has been seen occasionally from here.

In all some 200 species of wild flowers have been recorded. Some are exotic aliens that obviously grew from the garden soil that was dumped in the area. The rare Fuller's teasel *Dipsacus sativus* provides lots of seeds for the linnets and goldfinches which breed here, as does Wild fennel *Foeniculum vulgare*. Other unusual plants such as Hoary mustard *Hirschfeldia incana* arrived via Dublin Port as a contaminant from a grain crop. The Oxford Ragwort *Senecio squalidus* is another alien plant species found, and indeed, in many parts of Dublin City on waste ground. This species arrived in Cork in the early 1800s and travelled by train to Dublin in 1890, probably introduced with old building and railway materials. It remained near the railway at Inchicore for half a century until, during the second half of the twentieth century, it spread not only around Dublin city on waste soil, but journeyed with clinker and rubble from Inchicore to Wicklow, Belfast, Sligo, Dundalk, Coleraine and Waterford. It likes a slightly higher temperature than our normal ragwort *Senecio jacobaea*, so town and city life suits it.

The black and amber striped caterpillars of the Cinnabar moth adorn the stems and flowers of the Yellow ragwort, while the red and black colours of the flying adults warn predators that they taste nasty.

As you descend to the shore on route to the South Bull Wall keep an eye out for turnstones busily looking for food along the seaweed on the stony shore. They are particularly fond of Sandhoppers, which live and feed on the decomposing seaweeds.

• •

Cinnabar moth caterpillars, Irishtown Nature Park

THE SOUTH WALL

The Great South Wall (also known as South Bull Wall), built to keep sand from the South Bull mud flats from drifting into the River Liffey and silting it up, was completed towards the end of the eighteenth century. At the time it was one of the longest sea walls in the world at 3.5 miles long (5.6 kilometres). It cost about £200,000 to build and took 47 years, from 1748–1795. It was built of blocks of Dalkey granite, which were transported across the Bay in barges. Bullock Harbour, Coliemore Harbour and Sandycove Harbour were all constructed at this time to facilitate the loading of the granite blocks on to the barges. Dublin has retained all these amenities to the present day.

The walk down to the Poolbeg lighthouse gives a great view of the River Liffey as it enters the sea. Grey seals often swim up the Liffey and will surface for breath along the way, making them easily seen and recognised. In summer Black guillemots that breed in Dublin docks can be seen. At the very end where the river enters the bay, porpoises commonly occur. Indeed in July 2007 a pod of Bottle-nosed dolphins were observed in the water here just off the South Wall at the Shelley Banks.

In winter this is a good spot to look out to sea for Sea-ducks such as scoters, eiders, Long-tailed ducks, Red-breasted merganser and scaup, as well as divers and grebes.

The South Wall

COMMON AND ARCTIC TERNS

Common and Arctic terns can also be observed from the South Wall. At the mouth of the River Liffey, at the Pigeon House harbour, are two cold-water intakes – called dolphins – for the power station. One is wooden and one is concrete. These have been used as breeding sites in recent times by Common terns and Arctic terns – over 400 pairs (mostly Common) nested there in 2007. The dolphins are designated as proposed Natural Heritage Areas (pNHAs).

CROSSING THE LIFFEY

Back in the DART, the Liffey is crossed upstream from the coast via the Loop Line Bridge. The last glimpses of the Bay for the DART traveller are obtained as the DART travels through Fairview Park and crosses the Clontarf Road after Clontarf station. It follows an inland route after that until it reaches Sutton station where the view is northwards along the coast rather than south into the Bay. To continue the odyssey along the coast the traveller must part company with the DART at Clontarf station and proceed along the path between the Clontarf Road and the sea.

Main image: Wooden bridge to Bull Island
Inset: Black guillemot, Custom House Quay by the IFSC

Aerial shot of Bull Island

BULL ISLAND

Bull Island can be reached from Clontarf via a wooden bridge. In front you will see a spectacular view of the Dublin Mountains and Howth Head to your left.

Bull Island is the sea's gift to the people of Dublin. It is only in existence since the late 1820s – it is not yet 200 years old. It began to grow when the North Bull Wall was built in 1825 to improve Dublin Port. While the South Wall had helped somewhat, the size of ships had increased since then. They were not able to get over the bar, a large sandbank that formed where the River Liffey met the Irish Sea and dumped the load of sediment it accumulated along its length as it flowed. The North Bull Wall kept the channel free of sediment by changing the speed and direction of the currents in the bay. The sediments began to accumulate north of the new wall and in no time at all Bull Island rose out of the sea in the form of a line of sand dunes. By the late 1830s a second line had arisen parallel to the first. It now measures 5 kilometres by 1 kilometre and is inter-

nationally important as a wildlife area.

Tidal currents move very slowly between the island and the mainland, so can drop their load of very fine particles of mud and silt. As a result, this side of the island is where the mudflats and saltmarshes are. This area is defined by the fact that it is covered by salt water either daily, monthly or at least annually. Few species of plants or invertebrates can put up with this inundation of salt water, but those that can occur here in abundance.

Go out on to the mudflats and grab a handful of mud. It will contain lots of one species of snail that occurs here in abundance, the Laver spire shell *Hydrobia ulvae*. Each snail is very small – the shell barely reaches 0.6 centimetres in length, the size of a big grain of rice, but it occurs in densities of up to 60,000 per square metre because it can make a living here when hardly any other species can. The very fine mud particles would block the feeding and respiratory organs of most things, but this snail is able to manage. It burrows into the mud at low tide and rises as the tide comes in to feed on the algae and organic detritus brought in by the tide.

The other species here in the mud in abundance is a shrimp-like creature, an amphipod called *Corophium volutator*. This creature resides in a burrow 10 centimetres down, where it cowers when the tide is out. When it is safely covered by the tide it emerges to walk along the surface of the mud – a most peculiar looking creature indeed which seems to have about eight pairs of legs of varying lengths, and several abdominal appendages that don't qualify to be called legs. As it walks over the mud, it picks up edible fragments with its first pair of legs. The abdominal appendages, which are much shorter, work furiously to draw a current of water for respiration, and all the while the shrimp is balancing and actually walking on its last pair of legs, which are much longer than any other pair. Talk about multi-tasking! These shrimps are not above gobbling a ragworm (or two) if they happen on them during their peregrinations over the soft mud.

And it is the ability of these two species to live here in such numbers that makes this place so immensely important as an SPA – because they are the food for thousands and thousands of wading birds that flock here, particularly in winter when much of mainland Europe is frozen. Bull Island regularly supports in excess of 20,000 waders. Waders are wonderfully adapted to feed on such rich mudflats. They have long bills for probing the mud and long legs to wade in the mud and shallow incoming tide. Sixteen species of waders were recorded here during the winter of 2006/2007. So many different species can feed here together because the length of their bills and feet are different for each species so they can feed at different depths and not compete with each other. The curlew has the longest bill, so long, in fact, that it has a nerve running down to the tip so that it can feel what is happening in the mud below. Its curved beak allows it to comb a larger area per thrust than if the bill was straight. Such a long bill is matched with long legs. At the other end of the scale small waders, such as dunlin, probe with quick thrusts of their short bills (like so many sewing machines). Great flocks of these wheel and turn over the marshes, reflecting flashes of white in the low winter sunshine.

Over the winter of 2005/06 and 2006/07 the following waders were recorded by the Irish Wetlands Bird Survey (Dublin Bay Group)

Little egret	Snipe	
Oystercatcher	Black-tailed godwit	
Ringed plover	Bar-tailed godwit	
Golden plover	**Whimbrel**	
Grey plover	Curlew	
Lapwing	**Spotted redshank**	
Knot	Redshank	
Sanderling	Greenshank	
Dunlin	Turnstone	

KEY

PINK MEANS OCCURS IN NATIONALLY IMPORTANT NUMBERS

GREEN MEANS OCCURS IN INTERNATIONALLY IMPORTANT NUMBERS

From left to right: Ringed plover, curlew, oystercatcher and knot

There is great feeding here too in winter for wildfowl – swans, geese and ducks. Many of these birds are vegetarian and breed in the high Arctic, where they can feed on vegetation with their rapidly growing young for twenty-four hours a day if necessary, because there is continuous daylight. In winter, however, the vegetation is covered with snow and ice so they migrate south to unfrozen Ireland to over-winter (that is, spend the winter here feeding but not breeding). This is the top site in Ireland for the light-bellied Brent goose, which over-winters here in numbers of international importance. They feed by walking along the shoreline and mudflats, picking up vegetation, and by upending (stretching down with their long necks while their rear ends point up in the air) in the water to reach plants deeper down.

Eight species of duck were recorded here during the winter of 2006/2007, most of them in nationally important numbers. Wigeon, teal, pintail and shoveller rarely breed in this country but great flocks of them come to these mudflats in winter from mainland Europe. The handsome shelduck is the largest duck out on the mudflats. Goldeneye and red-breasted mergansers are more likely to be seen on the water as they feed by diving for invertebrates.

Wildfowl recorded during winter 2005/2006

Mute swan

Light-bellied Brent goose

Shelduck

Wigeon

Teal

Mallard

Pintail

Shoveller

Goldeneye

Red-breasted merganser

KEY

■ NATIONALLY IMPORTANT NUMBERS

■ INTERNATIONALLY IMPORTANT NUMBERS

While it is always possible to see Grey herons waiting patiently in the muddy channels for a meal, a new arrival in recent years is the elegant Little egret. This bird from the heron family used to occur much further south in Europe. Now because of climate change, its distribution is spreading north on a European scale. First it came to Ireland just as a summer visitor. But in the 1990s it began to stay all the year round and started to breed along the south and east coast. Now it is easy to see Little egrets on the mud flats in winter – twenty-three were recorded in Dublin in 2005/2006 – a number of national importance.

BULL ISLAND IN SUMMER

It is an idyllic place for wild flowers in the months of May and June. The sand doesn't hold water very well and because there is little nitrogen in the soil, greedy heavy plants, like coarse grasses, do not grow very well. So wild flowers really do well here. The light sandy soil quickly warms up and the dunes are covered in masses of yellow and purple Wild pansy, lavender-coloured thyme, yellow Lady's bedstraw and white tiny clusters of eyebright. Legumes do particularly well here, as they are able to fix nitrogen directly from the atmosphere, which confers a competitive advantage on them. Among the members of the legume or Wild pea family are yellow Bird's foot trefoil, cerise-coloured Rest harrow, red, white and yellow Flowering clovers and pale-yellow Kidney vetch.

This is one of the best places in Dublin to see flowering orchids.

Bee orchid – in bloom at the beginning of June

Pyramidal orchid – in bloom at the end of June

Other orchids found here are: the Spotted orchid, Heath spotted orchid and the Early purple orchid.

Fresh water is rare in sand dunes, so if any occurs it means that conditions are right for more delicate plants. Down towards the northern end, fresh water springs come close to the surface and the area is known as the Alder Marsh. Here there is enough water for alder trees and for willow and on the edges of this marsh some uncommon flowers grow. Orchids grow well in these conditions and the types found are: Autumn lady tresses, Marsh helleborine, the Northern marsh orchid and Early purple orchid. Wild flowers also occur such as the dark-blue Devil's bit scabious, Yellow-wort, Autumn gentian and the pink Common centaury.

Be sure to notice the flowers on the salt-marsh on the land-ward side. The plants here have been growing all summer long before they form flowers. Most of their flowers are purple in colour, as purple is a pigment that needs the long days to develop. Sea lavender, Sea aster and Sea milkwort are abundant for a few weeks at the end of August and bring sheets of purple colour to the usually grey-green vegetation.

Walking on the dunes in summer is such a pleasure. The grasses that grow here are soft with elegant flowering stems. Look out for Quaking grass, the downy Oat grass and Red fescue. The air is filled with the song of the skylarks, who nest here on the ground. Meadow pipits occur here, as do stonechats as well as the more common blackbirds, wrens and thrushes. There is a colony of Sand martins here too, which breed successfully most summers. You might spot some birds of prey, such as kestrels, merlins and Peregrine falcons, which hunt over the area.

Bee orchid, Bull Island

Rabbits are here in abundance and are much despised by the golfers of the Royal Dublin Golf Club and St Anne's Golf Club. However, these golf clubs provide a refuge for the Irish hare, which is under great pressure elsewhere in Dublin County from the abundant human population.

A fox or two are also resident here, with dens among the scrubby shelter planted around the golf clubs' grounds. Bats, which breed in St Anne's Park across the way, hunt over the island on summer evenings and several species have been recorded here.

Down on the shore, near the northern tip of the island, is where the common seals haul out to have their pups. These seals make quite a sight in June and July as they seem to sunbathe on the sandy beaches. Little terns have nested here, up to relatively recently, and indeed may recolonise – if conditions are right.

Common spotted or[chid]

COASTAL BUTTERFLIES

There are about thirty-two species of butterflies on the Irish List – of these twenty-two have been recorded along the coastal stretch of Dublin Bay. Bull Island is a good place to visit to find butterflies on a sunny calm day in late spring and early summer. Each butterfly species has its own particular food plant, on which it feeds as a caterpillar. So on Bull Island the food plants of many of the uncommon butterflies grow on the grassy sand-dune area.

Blue butterflies such as the Common Blue, the rare Small Blue, and the more ubiquitous Holly Blue, which is also widespread in gardens in Dublin City, can be spotted on the island. Other butterflies that like coastal habitats are grass-feeding species such as the Grayling, the Ringlet and the Gatekeeper. It is a good place too to keep an eye out for migrant butterflies that fly in from Europe when the weather is warm in mid summer. Red Admirals and Painted Ladies are common every year and Clouded Yellows are seen more frequently now as global warming takes effect.

Sand dunes are good places to observe dayflying moths too. Cinnabar moths occur here, their black wings with red stripes warning birds of their nasty taste. This red and black coloration occurs in the Burnet moth too, the red colour being in the form of six

Common blue on ribworth, Bull Island

red spots on the black front wings. Burnet moths construct their cocoons on the swaying stems of the Marram grass to avoid being eaten by birds at this early stage in their development. Having a hairy coat is another defence against hungry birds. The common name for hairy caterpillars is 'Hairy Molly' and butterflies such as Small tortoiseshell and the peacock have such caterpillars. Some species of moth, however, have brought this form of protection to a high art, for example, the caterpillar of the Garden tiger moth.

• •

Right: Adult Cinnabar moth
Below: Tiger moth caterpillar, Bull Island

THE NORTH BULL MOUSE

In 1895 there was great scientific excitement when H. Lyster Jameson, an eminent zoologist of the day, discovered sandy-coloured house mice on Bull Island. While walking among the dunes he noticed very pale sandy-coloured mice, which seemed to him to be the exact colour of the sand. The theory of natural selection being relatively new at the time, he concluded that here was a prime example of a mouse that had adapted to its environment. Normal grey-coloured mice would easily be seen and captured by kestrels and short-eared owls. Sandy ones had an advantage, by being difficult to see, and so they survived and left large numbers of progeny. He succeeded in trapping thirty-six house mice, whose colour varied from the usual grey right along a continuum to sandy. He removed the skins and deposited them in the Natural History museum, where they were labelled as a separate sub-species *Mus musculus jamesoni* the North Bull Island house mouse.

In 1931 Eugene O'Mahony, a biologist who worked in the Natural History Museum and who was familiar with the Bull Island mouse skins, set out to trap some more of them. But he could only trap field mice, a different species that had not been there in Jameson's time, and which were not sandy-coloured. He did however catch sandy-coloured house mice – exactly the same as those Bull Island ones – in mainland Sutton and Kilbarrack, where there was no sand. Eventually in 1935 he succeeded in catching four house mice on Bull Island, all with sandy-coloured coats.

In the early 1960s two eminent zoologists, Fergus O'Gorman and Azzo von Rezzori, went in pursuit of sandy mice again. They trapped thirty house mice on Bull Island – not one of which could be described as looking like the sandy-coloured ones collected by Jameson. James Fairley, a University College Galway zoologist, looked at the variation in colour in house mice on the east coast of Dublin in 1970, and came to the conclusion that no sub-species of *Mus musculus* – the house mouse, exists in Ireland. Colour is a very variable trait and can range from pure black, through grey and brown to biscuit, orange grey and pale orange. They are all the same species and can interbreed freely. So, there is in fact no Bull Island sandy-coloured house mouse. A pity really!

• • • • • • • •
Mouse

SUTTON

From the beach at Sutton there is a wonderful view of Bull Island and Howth Head – a good place to end our scenic journey on the DART. This beach carries a high tide line of washed-up seaweed and a good selection of the shells of the creatures that live in the Bay.

One shell you will not find here is that of the Dublin Bay Prawn – a misnamed species if ever there was one.

THE DUBLIN BAY PRAWN

You would think that the Dublin Bay prawn is the prime example of a wildlife species that was called after the place it was discovered. You might even think that Dublin Bay must be full of such delicacies. Well you'd be completely wrong. The Dublin Bay prawn is not actually a prawn, and it never lived in Dublin Bay. It is more like a small lobster with large front claws and a hard pink back shell over its tail. Familiar as we are with freshwater shellfish from the Far East, we know that real prawns have a soft and transparent polythene-like shell and no long front claws. In fact another name for the Dublin Bay prawn – called *Nephrops norvegicus* in Latin – is the Norway lobster, or scampi in Italian.

So where did this Dublin moniker come from? These shellfish live in burrows 50 metres below the sea – a depth not achieved anywhere in Dublin Bay. They are hunted by cod, ray and dogfish and caught by fishermen with bottom trawling nets. They occur in the Irish Sea, north of Lambay Island, off the coast of Meath and Louth, and further north as well. Howth, Clogherhead and Skerries are where they are landed now, but fishing boats fishing out of Dublin Bay and returning to Dublin Port with their catch originally caught them and so they were called 'Dublin Bay prawns'. They do actually occur on the west coast of Ireland too, and all the way from Iceland to Morocco, but the name persists, even if the geography and postal address is actually scientifically incorrect.

It is a tasty and popular item of food and is a valuable part of the Irish fish catch. In 2006, the most recent year for which figures are available, the Irish seafood exports in total were worth €362 million. Of this, the Dublin Bay prawn catch was worth €46 million. It is subject to EU quotas to prevent overfishing.

Dublin Bay prawn, ymount

A FINAL WORD

Dublin is home to a fascinating array of flora and fauna, so get out there and find out for yourself. Take a trip on the DART, or go for a walk along one of our capital's rivers, canals or parks. You never know, you might just enjoy sampling the 'wilder' side of Dublin!

APPENDIX

CHECKLIST

Terrestrial mammals

Hedgehog	*Erinaceus europaeus*
Pygmy shrew	*Sorex minutus*
Whiskered bat	*Myotis mystacinus*
Daubenton's bat	*Myotis daubentoni*
Leisler's bat	*Nyctalus leisleri*
Long-eared bat	*Plecotus auritus*
Common pipistrelle	*Pipistrellus pipistrellus*
Soprano pipistrelle	*Pipistrellus pygmaeus*
Nathusius pipistrelle	*Pipistrellus nathusii*
Natterer's bat	*Myotis nattereri*
Rabbit	*Oryctolagus cuniculus*
Irish hare	*Lepus timidus*
Red squirrel	*Sciurus vulgaris*
Grey squirrel	*Sciurus carolinensis*
Field mouse	*Apodemus sylvaticus*
House mouse	*Mus musculus*
Black rat	*Rattus rattus*
Brown rat	*Rattus norvegicus*
Fox	*Vulpes vulpes*
Stoat	*Mustela erminea*
American mink	*Mustela vison*
Badger	*Meles meles*
Otter	*Lutra lutra*
Feral goat	*Capra spp.*
Fallow deer	*Dama dama*

Marine mammals

Common seal	*Phoca vitulina*
Grey seal	*Halichoerus grypus*
Minke whale	*Balaenoptera acutorostrata*
Harbour porpoise	*Phocaena phocaena*
Common dolphin	*Delphinus delphis*
Bottle-nosed dolphin	*Tursiops truncatus*

Birds

Red-throated diver
Black-throated diver
Great Northern diver
Little grebe
Great crested grebe
Red-necked grebe
Slavonian grebe
Black-necked grebe
Fulmar
Sooty shearwater
Manx shearwater
Balearic shearwater
Storm petrel
Gannet
Cormorant
Shag
Little egret
Grey heron
Mute swan
Whooper swan
Pink-footed goose
White-fronted goose
Greylag goose
Canada goose
Barnacle goose
Brent goose
Common shelduck
Wigeon
American wigeon
Gadwall
Common teal
Green-winged teal
Mallard
Pintail
Garganey
Blue-winged teal
Shoveler

Pochard
Ring-necked duck
Tufted duck
Scaup
Lesser scaup
Eider
Long-tailed duck
Common scoter
Surf scoter
Velvet scoter
Common goldeneye
Smew
Red-breasted merganser
Goosander
Ruddy duck
Marsh harrier
Hen harrier
Goshawk
Sparrowhawk
Buzzard
Osprey
Kestrel
Merlin
Hobby
Peregrine
Pheasant
Water rail
Moorhen
Coot
Oystercatcher
Black-winged stilt
Avocet
Little ringed plover
Ringed plover
Dotterel
American golden plover
European golden plover

Grey plover
Lapwing
Knot
Sanderling
Little stint
White-rumped sandpiper
Baird's sandpiper
Pectoral sandpiper
Curlew sandpiper
Purple sandpiper
Dunlin
Buff-breasted sandpiper
Ruff
Jack snipe
Common snipe
Eurasian woodcock
Black-tailed godwit
Bar-tailed godwit
Whimbrel
Curlew
Spotted redshank
Common redshank
Greenshank
Lesser yellowlegs
Green sandpiper
Wood sandpiper
Common sandpiper
Turnstone
Grey phalarope
Pomarine skua
Arctic skua
Long-tailed skua
Great skua
Mediterranean gull
Little gull
Sabine's gull
Black-headed gull
Ring-billed gull
Common gull
Lesser black-backed gull
Herring gull
Yellow-legged gull
Iceland gull
Glaucous gull

Great black-backed gull
Kittiwake
Sandwich tern
Roseate tern
Common tern
Arctic tern
Forster's tern
Little tern
Whiskered tern
Black tern
White-winged black tern
Common guillemot
Razorbill
Black guillemot
Little auk
Puffin
Rock dove
Stock dove
Woodpigeon
Collared dove
Turtle dove
Cuckoo
Barn owl
Long-eared owl
Short-eared owl
Swift
Kingfisher
Skylark
Sand martin
Barn swallow
House martin
Meadow pipit
Rock pipit
Yellow wagtail
Grey wagtail
Pied wagtail
Waxwing
Dipper
Wren
Dunnock
Robin
Common redstart
Black redstart
Whinchat

Stonechat
Wheatear
Ring ouzel
Blackbird
Fieldfare
Song thrush
Redwing
Mistle thrush
Grasshopper warbler
Sedge warbler
Reed warbler
Lesser whitethroat
Common whitethroat
Garden warbler
Blackcap
Yellow-browed warbler
Wood warbler
Chiffchaff
Willow warbler
Goldcrest
Firecrest
Spotted flycatcher
Pied flycatcher
Long-tailed tit
Coal tit
Blue tit
Great tit
Treecreeper
Jay
Magpie
Jackdaw
Rook
Hooded crow
Carrion crow
Raven
Starling
House sparrow
Tree sparrow
Chaffinch
Brambling
Greenfinch
Goldfinch
Siskin
Linnet

Twite
Redpoll
Crossbill
Bullfinch
Lapland bunting
Snow bunting
Yellowhammer
Reed bunting

Freshwater fish

Salmon	*Salmo salar*
Sea trout	*Salmo trutta*
Brown trout	*Salmo trutta*
Eel	*Anguilla anguilla*
Three-spined stickleback	*Gasterosteus aculeatus*
Minnow	*Phoxinus phoxinus*
Stone loach	*Noemacheilus barbatulus*
Brook lamprey	*Lampetra planeri*
River lamprey	*Lampetra fluviatilis*
Perch	*Perca fluviatilis*
Roach	*Rutilus rutilus*
Rudd	*Scardinius erythrophthalmus*
Pike	*Esox lucius*
Tench	*Tinca tinca*
Carp	*Cyprinus carpio*
Bream	*Abramis brama*

Butterflies

Speckled wood	*Pararge aegeria*
Wall brown	*Pararge megera*
Grayling	*Eumenis semele*
Gatekeeper	*Maniola tithonius*
Meadow brown	*Maniola jurtina*
Small heath	*Coenonympha pamphilus*
Ringlet	*Aphantopus hyperantus*
Dark-green fritillary	*Argynnis aglaia*
Silver-washed fritillary	*Argynnis paphia*
Small tortoiseshell	*Aglais urticae*
Peacock	*Nymphalis io*
Small blue	*Cupido minimus*
Common blue	*Polyommatus icarus*
Holly blue	*Celastrina agriolus*
Small copper	*Lycaena phlaeas*
Wood white	*Leptidea sinapis*
Large white	*Pieris brassicae*
Small white	*Pieris rapae*
Green-veined white	*Pieris napi*
Orange tip	*Anthocharis cardamines*
Brimstone	*Gonepteryx rhamni*
Dingy skipper	*Erynnis tages*
Red admiral	*Vanessa atalanta*
Painted lady	*Cynthia cardui*
Clouded yellow	*Colias crocus*

Dragonflies

English names after *The Natural History of Ireland's Dragonflies*, Brian Nelson and Robert Thompson (2004) Ulster Museum

Amber-winged hawker	*Aeshna grandis*
Moorland hawker	*Aeshna juncea*
Spring hawker	*Brachytron pratense*
Vagrant emperor	*Hemianax ephippiger*
Four-spotted chaser	*Libellula quadrimaculata*
Common darter	*Sympetrum striolatum*

Damselflies

Banded jewelwing	*Calopteryx splendens*
Common spreadwing	*Lestes sponsa*
Azure bluet	*Coenagrion puella*
Variable bluet	*Coenagrion pulchellum*
Common bluet	*Enallagma cyathigerum*
Common bluetip	*Ischnura elegans*
Small bluetip	*Ischnura pumilio*
Spring redtail	*Pyrrhosoma nymphula*

Woodlice

Latin names only (no English names)

Androniscus dentiger
Trichoniscoides sarsi
Trichoniscus pusillus
Trichoniscus pygmaeus
Haplophthalmus danicus
Haplophthalmus mengei
Ligia oceanica
Philoscia muscorum
Oniscus asellus (often called Common woodlice)
Cylisticus convexus
Metoponorthus cingendus
Metoponorthus pruinosus
Porcellio laevis
Porcellio dilatatus
Porcellio spinicornis
Porcellio scaber
Eluma purpurascens
Armadillidium nasatum
Armadillidium vulgare (often called Pill woodlice)

BIBLIOGRAPHY

Asher, J et al, *The Millennium Atlas of Butterflies in Britain and Ireland*, Oxford, Oxford University Press, 2001.

Campbell, A, *Hamlyn Guide to the Sea shore and Shallow Seas of Britain and Europe*, London, Hamlyn Publishing Group, 1976.

Carey, M, Hamilton, H, Poole, A and Lawton, C, *The Irish Squirrel Survey*, 2007, Dublin, Coford, 2007.

Colgan, N, *Flora of the County Dublin*, Dublin, Hodges Figgis, 1904.

Collins, R and Whelan, J, *The Mute Swan in Dublin*, Irish Birds, 4; 181-202, 1990.

Dempsey, E and O'Clery, M, *Finding Birds in Ireland – the complete guide,* Dublin, Gill and Macmillan, 2007.

Dempsey, E and O'Clery, M, *The Complete Guide to Ireland's Birds*, Dublin, Gill and Macmillan, 2002.

Doogue, D and Harding, P, *Distribution Atlas of Woodlice in Ireland*, Dublin, An Foras Forbartha, 1982.

Dublin City Council, *Dublin City Biodiversity Action Plan 2007-2010*, Dublin, 2007.

Dublin Naturalists' Field Club, *A Supplement to Colgan's Flora of the County Dublin*, Dublin, The Stationery Office, 1961.

Dublin Naturalists' Field Club, *Flora of County Dublin, Dublin Naturalists' Field Club*, Dublin Naturalists' Field Club, 1998.

Fairley, J, *A Critical re-appraisal of the status in Ireland of the eastern house mouse*, Mus musculus orientalis, Cretzmar. Irish Naturalists' Journal, 17:2-5, 1971.

Giraldus Cambrensis, *Topographia Hibernica*, 1187.

Gogarty, O, *Selected Poems*, New York, Macmillan Company, 1933.

Grahame, Kenneth, *The Wind in the Willows*, London, Penguin Classics, 2005.

Hayden, T and Harrington, R, *Exploring Irish Mammals*, Dublin, Town House, 2000.

Healy, E, Moriarty, C and O'Flaherty, G, *The Book of the Liffey from source to the sea*, Dublin, Wolfhound Press, 1988.

How, W, *Phytologia Britannica*, London, 1650.

Joyce, J, A, *Ulysses*, Paris, Shakespeare and Company, 1922.

Mackay, J, *Flora Hibernica*, Dublin, 1836.

Moore, D and More, A, *Cybele Hibernica*, Dublin, 1866.

Moriarty, C, *Down the Dodder*, Dublin, Wolfhound Press, 1991.

Moriarty, C, *Exploring Dublin, Wildlife, Parks, Waterways*, Dublin, Wolfhound Press, 1997.

Nelson, B and Thompson, R, *The Natural History of Ireland's Dragonflies*, Belfast, Ulster Museum, 2004.

Ní Lamhna, É, *Provisional Atlas of Dragonflies in Ireland*, Dublin, An Foras Forbartha, 1978.

Ní Lamhna, É, *Provisional Distribution Atlas of Butterflies in Ireland*, Dublin, An Foras Forbartha, 1980.

Ní Lamhna, É, *Provisional Distribution Atlas of Amphibians, Reptiles and Mammals in Ireland*, Dublin, An Foras Forbartha, 1983.

Ní Lamhna, É, *An Air Quality Survey of Dublin City*, Dublin, An Foras Forbartha, 1988.

O'Connor, J and Ashe, P, *Irish Indoor Insects*, Dublin, Town House, 2000.

Praeger, R L, *The Way that I Went*, Dublin, Hodges Figgis & Co, 1937.

Rutty, J, *An Essay towards a natural history of the county of Dublin*, Dublin, W. Sleater, 1772.

Tree Council of Ireland, *Champion Trees – A Selection of Ireland's Great Trees*, Dublin, Tree Council of Ireland, 2005.

Threlkeld, Caleb, *Synopsis Stirpium Hibernicarum*, Dublin, 1762.

Wilson F, Goodbody, R and Nairn, R, *Dublin City Graveyards Study – a report for Dublin City Council*, 2004.

Wilson, J and Berrow, S, *A guide to the identification of the Whales and Dolphins of Ireland*, Irish Whale and Dolphin Group, 2007.

Wyse Jackson, P and Sheehy Skeffington, M, *The Flora of Inner Dublin*, Royal Dublin Society, 1884.

Websites

Bat website: www.batconservationireland.org

Fishing website: www.fishingireland.net

Bird website: www.birdwatchireland.ie

INDEX